THE INTOLERANCE OF TOLERANCE

The Intolerance of Tolerance

D. A. CARSON

WILLIAM B. EERDMANS PUBLISHING COMPANY
GRAND RAPIDS, MICHIGAN / CAMBRIDGE, U.K.

Published 2012 by

Wm. B. Eerdmans Publishing Co.

2140 Oak Industrial Drive N.E., Grand Rapids, Michigan 49505 /

P.O. Box 163, Cambridge CB3 9PU U.K.

Printed in the United States of America

18 17 16 15 14 13 12   7 6 5 4 3 2 1

Library of Congress Cataloging-in-Publication Data

Carson, D. A.

The intolerance of tolerance / D. A. Carson.

p.   cm.

Includes indexes.

ISBN 978-0-8028-3170-5 (cloth: alk. paper)

1. Toleration — Religious aspects — Christianity.

2. Religious tolerance — Christianity.

3. Christianity and other religions.   I. Title.

BR1610.C325   2012

261.7′2 — dc23

2011027511

www.eerdmans.com

for
Graham Cole
with thanks for
many stimulating conversations

Contents

—⟨⟩⟨⟩⟨⟩—

Preface

—◦◦◦◦—

Several times during the last ten years or so I have been invited to give a "public lecture" at one university or another. These invitations arise when a university has set aside a sum of money to pay for the travel expenses and honorarium of someone nominated by a recognized university student group to come and give an address on some topic of public interest. For example, the local physics club may bring in a notable theoretical physicist to give a public lecture on the latest developments in the world of quarks. My invitations have come when a recognized student Christian group has made application to these funds and their proposal has been accepted. The possible topics are extremely wide-ranging. It is usually understood that the lectures are not to be overtly religious. The numbers who attend may vary from a handful to many hundreds, depending almost entirely on either the interest generated by the topic or the reputation of the lecturer, or both.

When it has been my turn, I have three times announced as my title the title of this book, "The Intolerance of Tolerance." In each case the crowd that showed up was surprisingly large, and with a greater percentage of faculty attending than is usually the case. Believe me when I say that the reputation of the lecturer had nothing to do with the attendance: it was the topic alone that drew people. I ended each of these talks by stating my own convictions as a Christian and trying to show what bearing biblically faithful Christianity has on the subject. In each case I allowed time for Q & A; in each case these exchanges were vigorous, courteous, sometimes amusing, and certainly (from my perspective) enjoyable.

All of this is a roundabout way of mentioning one of the streams that brought me to write this book. These occasional lectures have kept me reading about and thinking through this topic, and it is high time I set some of this down in book form. It does not take much cultural awareness to see that the difficulties surrounding this subject are eating away at both Western Christianity and the fabric of Western culture. The challenges before us are not going to go away any time soon.

The second stream was my book *Christ and Culture Revisited* (also published by Eerdmans). That book provides more biblical reflection and theology, but it more or less covers the waterfront: I tried to think about culture in pretty broad terms. By contrast, the topic of this present book is much more narrowly focused. As I wrote the earlier one, however, I kept noting subtopics that cried out for more detailed unpacking — and none more so than tolerance/intolerance. What you now hold in your hand is the result. Perhaps I may be forgiven if from time to time I refer back to *Christ and Culture Revisited* to provide the underpinnings for some of my arguments here.

Once again I am grateful to Andy Naselli, my very able assistant, for making helpful suggestions and for compiling the indexes.

D. A. CARSON

ONE

Introduction:
The Changing Face of Tolerance

—⟨ɷɷ⟩—

To speak of "the intolerance of tolerance" might strike some people as nothing more than arrant nonsense — an obscure oxymoron, perhaps, as meaningless as talk about the hotness of cold or the blackness of white. Tolerance currently occupies a very high place in Western culture, a bit like motherhood and apple pie in America in the early 1950s: it is considered rather gauche to question it. To hint, as my title does, that this tolerance might itself on occasion be *in*tolerant is unlikely to win many friends. To put the matter in a slightly more sophisticated way, tolerance has become part of the Western "plausibility structure." As far as I know, the expression "plausibility structure" was coined by sociologist Peter L. Berger.[1] He uses it to refer to structures of thought widely and almost unquestioningly accepted throughout a particular culture. One of his derivative arguments is that in tight, monolithic cultures (e.g., Japan), the reigning plausibility structures may be enormously complex — that is, there may be many interlocking stances that are widely assumed and almost never questioned. By contrast, in a highly diverse culture like what dominates many nations in the Western world, the plausibility structures are necessarily more restricted, for the very good reason

---

1. See his *The Sacred Canopy: Elements of a Sociological Theory of Religion* (New York: Doubleday, 1967).

that there are fewer stances held in common.[2] The plausibility structures that *do* remain, however, tend to be held with extra tenacity, almost as if people recognize that without such structures the culture will be in danger of flying apart. And tolerance, I am suggesting, is, in much of the Western world, part of this restricted but tenaciously held plausibility structure. To saunter into the public square and question it in some way or other not only is to tilt at windmills but is also culturally insensitive, lacking in good taste, boorish.

But I press on regardless, persuaded that the emperor has no clothes, or, at best, is sporting no more than Jockey shorts. The notion of tolerance is changing, and with the new definitions the shape of tolerance itself has changed. Although a few things can be said in favor of the newer definition, the sad reality is that this new, contemporary tolerance is intrinsically intolerant. It is blind to its own shortcomings because it erroneously thinks it holds the moral high ground; it cannot be questioned because it has become part of the West's plausibility structure. Worse, this new tolerance is socially dangerous and is certainly intellectually debilitating. Even the good that it wishes to achieve is better accomplished in other ways. Most of the rest of this chapter is devoted to unpacking and defending this thesis.

The Old Tolerance and the New

Let's begin with dictionaries. In the *Oxford English Dictionary,* the first meaning of the verb "to tolerate" is "To endure, sustain (pain or hardship)." That usage is becoming obsolete, but it still surfaces today when we say that a patient has a remarkable ability to tolerate pain. The second meaning: "To allow to exist or to be done or practised without authoritative interference or molestation; also *gen.* to allow, permit." Third: "To bear without repugnance; to allow intellectually, or in taste, sentiment, or principle; to put up with." Webster's *Unabridged Dictionary* is similar: "1. to allow; permit; not interfere with.

2. Peter L. Berger, *The Heretical Imperative: Contemporary Possibilities of Religious Affirmation* (Garden City: Doubleday, 1979).

2. to recognize and respect (others' beliefs, practices, etc.) without necessarily agreeing or sympathizing. 3. to put up with; to bear; as, he *tolerates* his brother-in-law. 4. in medicine, to have tolerance for (a specified drug, etc.)." Even the computer-based dictionary *Encarta* includes in its list "ACCEPT EXISTENCE OF DIFFERENT VIEWS to recognize other people's right to have different beliefs or practices without an attempt to suppress them." So far so good: all these definitions are on the same page. When we turn to *Encarta*'s treatment of the corresponding noun "tolerance," however, a subtle change appears: "1. ACCEPTANCE OF DIFFERENT VIEWS the accepting of the differing views of other people, e.g., in religious or political matters, and fairness toward the people who hold these different views."

This shift from "accepting the existence of different views" to "acceptance of different views," from recognizing other people's right to have different beliefs or practices to accepting the differing views of other people, is subtle in form, but massive in substance.[3] To accept that a different or opposing position exists and deserves the right to exist is one thing; to accept the position itself means that one is no longer opposing it. The new tolerance suggests that actually accepting another's position means believing that position to be true, or at least as true as your own. We move from allowing the free expression of contrary opinions to the acceptance of all opinions; we leap from permitting the articulation of beliefs and claims with which we do not

---

3. I should add that there is not a straight line from earlier dictionaries to later dictionaries. For a start, several dictionaries make rather striking distinctions between the verb "to tolerate" and the noun "tolerance" and other cognates. The distinction noted above, in other words, is grounded in a remarkable shift in current popular usage, not yet always reflected in dictionaries, which tend to lag behind. But one can find essays more than a century old that presuppose the "new" definition of tolerance: e.g., in 1891 Bernard Lazare wrote an essay titled "On the Need for Intolerance," *Entretiens politiques et littéraires* 3 (1891); the English translation is available at http://www.marxists.org/reference/archive/lazare-bernard/1891/intolerance.htm (accessed 28 Dec. 2009). Assuming that "tolerance" is "the characteristic of ages without beliefs" (a view that sidles up to the "new" tolerance), Lazare was arguing for strong religious and political stances: if you have strong and informed views, it is a virtue to be "intolerant" — by which he did not mean the silencing of opponents, but the vigorous defense of your views such that you denounce opposing views as wrong. While Lazare calls this virtue "intolerance," provided one insists that opponents have the right to affirm their views one might argue that this is in fact the "older" tolerance!

agree to asserting that all beliefs and claims are equally valid. Thus we slide from the old tolerance to the new.

The problem of what "tolerance" means is in fact more difficult than these few comments on dictionary entries might suggest. For in contemporary usage, both meanings continue in popular use, and often it is unclear what the speaker or writer means. For instance, "She is a very tolerant person": does this mean she gladly puts up with a lot of opinions with which she disagrees, or that she thinks all opinions are equally valid? A Muslim cleric says, "We do not tolerate other religions": does this mean that, according to this cleric, Muslims do not think that other religions should be permitted to exist, or that Muslims cannot agree that other religions are as valid as Islam? A Christian pastor declares, "Christians gladly tolerate other religions": does this mean, according to the pastor, that Christians gladly insist that other religions have as much right to exist as Christianity does, or that Christians gladly assert that all religions are equally valid? "You Christians are so intolerant," someone asserts: does this mean that Christians wish all positions contrary to their own were extirpated, or that Christians insist that Jesus is the only way to God? The former is patently untrue; the latter is certainly true (at least, if Christians are trying to be faithful to the Bible): Christians *do* think that Jesus is the only way to God. But does that make them intolerant? In the former sense of "intolerant," not at all; the fact remains, however, that any sort of exclusive truth claim is widely viewed as a sign of gross intolerance. *But the latter depends absolutely on the second meaning of "tolerance."*

Other distinctions can be usefully introduced. Go back to the assertion "Christians gladly tolerate other religions." Let us assume for a moment that the *first* meaning of "tolerate" is in view — i.e., Christians gladly insist that other religions have as much right to exist as their own, however much those same Christians may think the other religions are deeply mistaken in some respects. Even this more classical understanding of "tolerate" and "tolerance" leaves room for a certain amount of vagueness. Does the statement envisage *legal* tolerance? In that case, it is affirming that Christians gladly fight for the equal standing before the law of all religious minorities.[4] Of course,

4. I learned this well from my father, who was one of the rare evangelicals who

4

from a Christian perspective, this is a temporary arrangement that lasts only until Christ returns. It is a way of saying that in this fallen and broken world order, in this time of massive idolatry, in this age of theological and religious confusion, God has so ordered things that conflict, idolatry, confrontation, and wildly disparate systems of thought, *even about God himself,* persist. In the new heaven and the new earth, God's desires will not be contested but will be the object of worshiping delight. For the time being, however, Caesar (read: government) has the responsibility to preserve social order in a chaotic world. Although Caesar remains under God's providential sovereignty, nevertheless there is a difference between God and Caesar — and Jesus himself has told us to render to Caesar what is Caesar's and to God what is God's.[5] It will not be like that in the new heaven and the new earth. Thus even this *legal* tolerance, which Christians should surely defend, belongs to the present, to the time when the kingdom of God has dawned but has not yet been consummated, or (to say it the way theologians do) to this age of inaugurated but not yet final eschatology.

Of course, in the right context the same sentence, "Christians gladly tolerate other religions," might suggest, not *legal* tolerance, but *social* tolerance: that is, in a multicultural society, people of different religions should mix together without slights and condescension, for all people have been made in the image of God and all will give an account to him on the last day. Of all people, Christians ought to know that they are not one whit socially superior to others. They talk about a great Savior, but they are not to think of themselves as a great people. So *social* tolerance should be encouraged.

Yet another distinction demands brief mention. Someone might assert that the God of the Bible, even under the terms of the new covenant, does not hold up tolerance as a virtue: if men and women do not repent and by conversion come under the Lordship of Christ, they perish. Certainly the God of the Bible does not hold up tol-

---

supported the right of Jehovah's Witnesses to freedom of worship and proselytism, at a time when the Duplessis government of Québec was oppressing them: see my *Memoirs of an Ordinary Pastor: The Life and Reflections of Tom Carson* (Wheaton: Crossway, 2008).

5. For a much fuller treatment of this point, see D. A. Carson, *Christ and Culture Revisited* (Grand Rapids: Eerdmans, 2008).

erance *in the second sense* as a virtue. Yet is not God's patience and forbearance in delaying Christ's return a form of tolerance, intended to lead people to repentance (Romans 2:4)? Hence the distinction: bad ideas and bad actions are tolerated (in the first sense), reluctantly and with bold articulation of what makes them bad, while the people who hold those bad ideas or perform those bad actions are tolerated (again, in the first sense) without any sense of begrudging reluctance, but in the hope that they will come to repentance and faith. Tolerance toward persons, in this sense, is surely a great virtue to be nurtured and cultivated.

These and other distinctions need to be thought through a little more; they will be picked up later in this book. At the moment it is more urgent to explore more thoroughly how widely different the old tolerance and the new tolerance really are.

Sharpening the Contrast between the Old Tolerance and the New

Under the older view of tolerance, a person might be judged tolerant if, while holding strong views, he or she insisted that others had the right to dissent from those views and argue their own cases. This view of tolerance is in line with the famous utterance often (if erroneously) assigned to Voltaire: "I disapprove of what you say, but I will defend to the death your right to say it."[6] This older view of tolerance makes three assumptions: (1) there is objective truth out there, and it is our duty to pursue that truth; (2) the various parties in a dispute think that they know what the truth of the matter is, even though they disagree sharply, each party thinking the other is wrong; (3) nevertheless they hold that the best chance of uncovering the truth of the matter, or the

---

6. Those exact words are not found in Voltaire's literary remains but first show up in a book by Evelyn Beatrice Hall writing under the pseudonym of Stephen G. Tallentyre, *The Friends of Voltaire* (London: Smith Elder & Co., 1906). Voltaire did nevertheless leave behind not a few memorable statements on tolerance, e.g., "What is tolerance? It is the consequence of humanity. We are all formed of frailty and error; let us pardon reciprocally each other's folly — that is the first law of nature" (the first line of his essay "Tolerance," 1755).

6

best chance of persuading most people with reason and not with coercion, is by the unhindered exchange of ideas, no matter how wrongheaded some of those ideas seem. This third assumption demands that all sides insist that their opponents must not be silenced or crushed. Free inquiry may eventually bring the truth out; it is likely to convince the greatest number of people. Phlogiston (an imaginary substance that chemists once thought to cause combustion) will be exposed, and oxygen will win; Newtonian mechanics will be bested, and Einsteinian relativity and quantum mechanics will both have their say.

One version of this older view of tolerance — one might call it the secular libertarian version — has another wrinkle to it. In his famous text on liberty, John Stuart Mill (1806-1873) opts for a secularist basis to tolerance. In the domain of religion, Mill argues, there are insufficient rational grounds for verifying the truth claims of any religion. The only reasonable stance toward religion is therefore public agnosticism and private benign tolerance. For Mill, people should be tolerant in the domain of religion, not because this is the best way to uncover the truth, but precisely because whatever the truth, there are insufficient means for uncovering it.[7]

A parable made famous by a slightly earlier thinker, Gotthold Ephraim Lessing (1729-1781), nicely illustrates this perspective.[8] Lessing sets the parable in the twelfth century during the Third Crusade. The setting is critical to understanding what Lessing was trying to establish by his parable. This setting is a conversation among three characters, each of whom represents one of the world's three monotheistic religions: Saladin, the Muslim sultan; Nathan the Wise, a Jew; and a Christian Knight Templar. Saladin says to Nathan, "You are so wise; now tell me, I entreat, what human faith, what theological law

---

7. John Stuart Mill, *On Liberty* (London: Longman, Roberts & Green, 1869). The book has been reprinted many times.

8. The parable appears in *Nathan the Wise,* the last play written by Lessing. The German edition from which the English translation was first made was published in 1868 (Leipzig: Tauchnitz). The play reworks the parable of the three rings, which first appears in the fourteenth century in Boccaccio's *Decameron.* For background to the parable, see Alan Mittleman, "Toleration, Liberty, and Truth: A Parable," *Harvard Theological Review* 95 (2002): 353-72. The English translation I have used is Lessing's *Nathan the Wise,* trans. Patrick Maxwell, ed. George Alexander Kohut (New York: Bloch, 1939).

hath struck you as the truest and the best?"[9] Instead of answering directly, Nathan tells his parable. A man owned an opal ring of superlative beauty and extraordinary, not to say magical, powers. Whoever wore it was beloved by God and by human beings. He had received it from his father, who had received it from his, and so on — it had been passed down from generation to generation, from time immemorial. The man with the ring had three sons, each of whom he loved equally, and to each of whom he promised, at one time or another, that he would give the ring. Approaching death, the man realized, of course, that he could not make good on his promises, so he secretly asked a master jeweler to make two perfect copies of the ring. The jeweler did such a magnificent job that the rings were physically indistinguishable, even though only one had the magical powers. Now on his deathbed, the man called each of his sons individually to his side and gave him a ring. The man died, and only then did his sons discover that each of the sons had a ring. They began to argue about which one now possessed the original magic ring. In the play, Nathan the Wise describes their bickering and comments:

> [The brothers] investigate, recriminate, and wrangle all in vain
> Which was the true original genuine ring
> Was undemonstrable
> Almost as much as now by us is undemonstrable
> The one true faith.[10]

Wanting to resolve their dispute, the brothers ask a wise judge to settle the issue, but his ruling refuses to discriminate:

> If each of you in truth received his ring
> Straight from his father's hand, let each believe
> His own to be the true and genuine ring.[11]

The judge urges the brothers to abandon their quest to determine which ring is the magic original. Each brother should instead accept his ring as if it were the original and in that conviction live a life of

9. Lessing, *Nathan the Wise*, 243.
10. Lessing, *Nathan the Wise*, 249.
11. Lessing, *Nathan the Wise*, 252-53.

moral goodness. This would bring honor both to their father and to God.

Lessing's parable resonated with his eighteenth-century Enlightenment readers. The three great monotheistic religions were so similar that each group should happily go on thinking that their religion was the true one, and focus on lives of virtue and goodness, free of nasty dogmatism, the dogmatism that was blamed for the bloody wars of the previous century. What was called for, in other words, was religious tolerance. There is no harm in believing that your monotheistic religion is best, provided you live a good life and let others think that their religion is best.

Small wonder the parable retains its appeal to readers in the twenty-first century. People today are no less skeptical about claims to exclusive religious truth than were Lessing's readers. They will be inclined to think well of a religion if it produces morally respectable and religiously tolerant adherents. Today, of course, the parable would have to be revised: instead of three rings, we would need dozens of them, if not hundreds, to symbolize the mutual acceptability of the many religious options, whether monotheistic, polytheistic, or nontheistic. And, of course, we could not concede today, as Lessing could, that one of the rings really is the original.

In some ways, of course, Lessing's parable is not very satisfying. To make the parable "work," at least three rather ridiculous stances have been incorporated into the story. (1) The god-figure in the parable, the man with the magic ring, foolishly promises the ring to each of his three sons, even though he knows full well he cannot make good on his multiple promises. Far from loving his three sons equally, he is presented as a weak fool who makes impossible promises. This is not an incidental detail in the story; it is an essential component that sets up *why* the father goes to the trouble of deceiving at least two of his sons with fake rings. So has God made impossible and mutually conflicting promises to his disparate sons, ostensibly loving all of them so much he ends up lying to them? (2) The entire parable presupposes that we, the readers, know what God has done. Far from fostering a benign tolerance on the ground that we cannot know which ring is the original, this tolerance is in reality grounded in the dogmatic certainty that God himself has produced fake rings because he cannot bear to disappoint any of his sons. In other words, the story "works" only because the reader has this outsider's knowledge of what God has done. Far from advocating a certain kind of epistemological restraint grounded in our ignorance of what God is like, the parable assumes the reader knows *exactly* what God is like: he is the kind of father who happily creates counterfeit rings to keep his boys happy and in the dark. (3) Equally implausible in the story is the way in which the fake rings are physically indistinguishable from the genuine original, yet lacking in the original's power. If over time the original does not produce distinctive blessings owing to its magical properties, its magic is so weak as to be irrelevant. The counterfeits, in other words, are not only good copies physically, but they seem to work as well as the original provided each son *thinks* the copy is the original. In other words, we are taken away from a powerful religion that actually transforms people to multiple religions where it does not matter all that much whether one of them is truly powerful or not: what matters is that its defenders *think* it is powerful. The same problem faces the account of the dialogue between Timothy and the Muslim caliph of Baghdad about A.D. 800 — an account that Philip Jenkins has made popular:

> Consider the story told by Timothy, a patriarch of the Nestorian church. Around 800, he engaged in a famous debate with the Muslim caliph in Baghdad, a discussion marked by reason and civility on both sides. Imagine, Timothy said, that we are all in a dark house, and someone throws a precious pearl in the midst of a pile of ordinary stones. Everyone scrabbles for the pearl, and some think they've found it, but nobody can be sure until day breaks.
>
> In the same way, he said, the pearl of true faith and wisdom had fallen into the darkness of this transitory world; each faith believed that it alone had found the pearl. Yet all he could claim — and all the caliph could say in response — was that some faiths thought they had enough evidence to prove that they were indeed holding the real pearl, but the final truth would not be known in this world.[12]

12. "When Jesus Met Buddha," *Boston Globe* (14 December 2008), http://www
.boston.com/bostonglobe/ideas/articles/2008/12/14/when_jesus_met_buddha/, last
accessed 31 December 2009.

Once again, there is a precious pearl, but only one precious pearl. Under this narrative, the dawning light will expose the stones for what they are.

Still, even though Lessing's parable is riddled with conceptual problems, one understands how it made a powerful appeal in his day and continues to resonate with many readers in our postmodern world.

In one respect, however, Lessing's parable is not very contemporary. Both Mill and Lessing thought that there is objective truth out there (after all, there is at least one magic ring!), but their rationalist and secular presuppositions drove them to infer that at least in some domains the truth is not accessible. One can *think* that something or other is true, and *argue* the case, but if one cannot prove that this something is true in a manner that conforms to the verification standards of public science, the wisest stance is benign tolerance.

In other words, the older view of tolerance held *either* that truth is objective and can be known, and that the best way to uncover it is bold tolerance of those who disagree, since sooner or later the truth will win out; *or* that while truth can be known in some domains, it probably cannot be known in other domains, and that the wisest and least malignant course in such cases is benign tolerance grounded in the superior knowledge that recognizes our limitations. By contrast, the new tolerance argues that there is no one view that is exclusively true. Strong opinions are nothing more than strong preferences for a particular version of reality, each version equally true. Lessing wanted people to be tolerant because, according to him, we cannot be sure which ring is the magic one — but he did not deny that there is a magic ring. The new approach to tolerance argues that all the rings are equally magic. That means the reason for being tolerant is not that we cannot know which ring is magic, nor that this is the best way to find out which ring is magic, but rather that since all the rings are equally magic or non-magic it is irresponsible to suggest that any of the rings is merely a clever imitation without magical power. We must be tolerant, not because we cannot distinguish the right path from the wrong path, but because all paths are equally right.

If you begin with this new view of tolerance, and then elevate this view to the supreme position in the hierarchy of moral virtues, the supreme sin is *in*tolerance. The trouble is that such intolerance, like the new tolerance, also takes on a new definition. Intolerance is no longer a refusal to allow contrary opinions to say their piece in public, but must be understood to be any questioning or contradicting the view that all opinions are equal in value, that all worldviews have equal worth, that all stances are equally valid. To question such postmodern axioms is by definition intolerant.[13] For such questioning there is no tolerance whatsoever, for it is classed as intolerance and must therefore be condemned. It has become the supreme vice.

The importance of the distinction between the older view of tolerance and this more recent view cannot easily be exaggerated. I do not think that my summary of the new view of tolerance is exaggerated. In a much-quoted line, Leslie Armour, professor emeritus of philosophy at the University of Ottawa, writes, "Our idea is that to be a virtuous citizen is to be one who tolerates everything except intolerance."[14] The United Nations *Declaration of Principles on Tolerance* (1995) asserts, "Tolerance . . . involves the rejection of dogmatism and absolutism." But why? Might one not hold a certain dogma to be correct, to hold it absolutely, while insisting that others have the right to hold conflicting things to be dogmatically true? Indeed, does not the assertion "Tolerance . . . involves the rejection of dogmatism and absolutism" sound a little, well, dogmatic and absolute? Thomas A. Helmbock, executive vice president of the national Lambda Chi Alpha fraternity, writes, "The definition of the new tolerance is that every individual's beliefs, values, lifestyle, and perception of truth claims are equal. . . . There is no hierarchy of truth. Your beliefs and my beliefs

13. On postmodernism, see D. A. Carson, *The Gagging of God: Christianity Confronts Pluralism* (Grand Rapids: Zondervan, 1996); idem, "The SBJT Forum: What Positive Things Can Be Said about Postmodernism?" *Southern Baptist Journal of Theology* 5, no. 2 (2001): 94-96; idem, "The Dangers and Delights of Postmodernism," *Modern Reformation* 12, no. 4 (July-August 2003): 11-17; idem, "Maintaining Scientific and Christian Truths in a Postmodern World," in *Can We Be Sure about Anything? Science, Faith and Postmodernism* (Leicester: Inter-Varsity, 2005), 102-25.

14. When I say "much-quoted," I mean I have heard the statement on radio talk-shows (e.g., Bob Harvey) and read it in books (e.g., Josh McDowell and Bob Hostetler, *The New Tolerance: How a Cultural Movement Threatens to Destroy You* [Carol Stream: Tyndale House, 1998], 43).

are equal, and all truth is relative."[15] If, however, the new tolerance evaluates all values and beliefs as positions worthy of respect, one may reasonably ask if this includes Nazism, Stalinism, and child sacrifice — or, for that matter, the respective stances of the Ku Klux Klan and other assorted ethnic supremacist groups.

In the next chapter I collect a sample of current developments along these lines. For the moment, it is enough to observe that under the aegis of this new tolerance, no absolutism is permitted, except for the absolute prohibition of absolutism. Tolerance rules, except that there must be no tolerance for those who disagree with this peculiar definition of tolerance. As S. D. Gaede puts it:

> In the past, PC [= political correctness] generally centered on issues that were quite substantive. The Victorians were prudish about sex because they were enthusiastic about bourgeois morality. In the fifties, many Americans were intolerant of any notion that seemed remotely "pink" (socialistic) because they assumed communism to be a major threat to their economic and political freedom. Today's PC, however, is intolerant not of substance but of intolerance itself. Thus, although the politically correct world would have a great deal of difficulty agreeing on what constitutes goodness and truth, they have no trouble at all agreeing that intolerance itself is wrong. Why? Because no one deserves to be offended.[16]

Gaede's shrewd insight prompts three further clarifications that pave the way for discussion in later chapters.

First, both the old tolerance and the new have obvious limits. The old tolerance, for instance, will happily allow, say, Islam to be preached in a Western country that is minimally Muslim. It may go so far as to allow *militant* Islam to be preached, even while it detests the message. But obviously it will not allow militant Muslims to blow up people and buildings: there will be repercussions, and the violence will not be tolerated. In due course those who *advocate* such violent

---

15. "Insights on Tolerance," *Cross and Crescent* [publication of the Lambda Chi Alpha International Fraternity] (Summer 1996): 3.

16. S. D. Gaede, *When Tolerance Is No Virtue: Political Correctness, Multiculturalism and the Future of Truth and Justice* (Downers Grove: InterVarsity, 1993), 23.

actions may also find their freedom to speak curtailed. Again, the old tolerance will allow those who advocate euthanasia to propagate their views, even though most of those who defend the old tolerance think euthanasia is morally wrong. As long as laws about euthanasia stand on the books, however, they will prosecute those who practice it; they may even prosecute those who conspire to commit euthanasia in a particular instance (as opposed to advocating the practice in general terms). Similarly, the new tolerance might well prove very tolerant of all religions, but would worry about any religion that thinks it has some sort of exclusive path to salvation, and would certainly be opposed to any religion that advocates bombing its opponents.

Both the old tolerance and the new tolerance may actually share some limits: both, for instance, may tolerate the defense of homosexuality (though perhaps more in the first group will dislike what is being defended, while more in the second group will think homosexuality is harmless and may be a good thing), and both may even tolerate the *advocacy* (but not the practice) of pedophilia (because it judges the practice to be wrong). In other words, most in both camps will draw the line at the actual practice of pedophilia, or at the distribution of pedophilial pornography, not least because of the damage it does. So both the old tolerance and the new will use the specter of the person who falsely cries "Fire!" in a crowded theater as an example of where freedom of speech must be limited, where tolerance must not prevail. By and large, however, they do not think of tolerance in quite the same way (as we have seen), and very often they do not draw the limits of tolerance, however understood, in quite the same place.

More importantly, if Gaede's insight, referred to above, is right, the old tolerance draws its limits on the basis of substantive arguments about truth, goodness, doing harm, and protecting society and its victims, while the new tolerance draws its limits on the basis of what it judges to be intolerant, which has become the supreme vice. Advocates of the new tolerance often find no more scalding epithet to hurl at those with whom they disagree than "intolerant" and related categories: bigoted, narrow-minded, ignorant, and so forth. Advocates of the old tolerance rarely charge their opponents with intolerance (although that is exactly what this book is doing!); rather, their epithets are shaped by their perception of the evil that cannot be tolerated (so defenders of euthanasia are committing murder, suicide bombers are terrorists, and so forth).

The fact that the new tolerance is most prone to label all of its opponents intolerant leads to a *second* reflection. The charge of intolerance has come to wield enormous power in much of Western culture — at least as much as the charge of "communist" during the McCarthy years. It functions as a "defeater belief."[17] A defeater belief is a belief that defeats other beliefs — i.e., if you hold a defeater belief to be true (whether it is true or not is irrelevant), you cannot possibly hold certain other beliefs to be true: the defeater belief rules certain other beliefs out of court and thus defeats them. For instance, if you believe that there is no one way to salvation and that those who think there is only one way to salvation are ignorant and intolerant, then voices that insist Islam is the only way, or that Jesus is the only way, will not be credible to you: you will dismiss their beliefs as ignorant and intolerant, nicely defeated by your own belief that there cannot possibly be only one way to salvation. Your belief has defeated theirs.

So if a Christian articulates a well-thought-out exposition of who Jesus is and what he has done, including how his cross and resurrection constitute the only way by which human beings can be reconciled to God, the person who holds the defeater belief I've just described may listen with some intellectual interest but readily dismiss everything you say without much thought. Put together several such defeater beliefs and make them widely popular, and you have created an implausibility structure: opposing beliefs are thought so implausible as to be scarcely worth listening to, let alone compelling or convincing.

Put these last two reflections together and the scope of the challenge becomes daunting and alarming. The new tolerance tends to avoid serious engagement over difficult moral issues, analyzing almost every issue on the one axis tolerant/intolerant, excluding all others from the pantheon of the virtuous who do not align with this axis. Perhaps the saddest blind spot of all in this stance is the failure to recognize just how culturally driven this particular defeater belief is. For instance, in the Middle East almost no one holds to the belief that all

17. Tim Keller has popularized this terminology. See especially his *The Reason for God: Belief in an Age of Skepticism* (New York: Dutton, 2008).

religions are of equal value; few dispute the postulate that there is only one way. What that way is, of course, is disputed. Advocates of the new tolerance are inclined to look down on the assorted cultures of the Middle East, holding that if the people in that region were all as "tolerant" as the advocates of the new tolerance themselves, peace would reign triumphant. Meanwhile many citizens of the Middle East view the advocates of the new tolerance as effete people who hold nothing precious but material possessions, who cannot think deeply about right and wrong, about truth and error, let alone about God. Too few on both sides ponder how one might build a culture in which people may strongly disagree with one another over fundamentals *and still tolerate the opponents because they are human beings made in the image of God.*

Third, granted that both the old tolerance and the new set limits to tolerance, not for a moment am I suggesting that the old tolerance always got things right while the new tolerance always gets things wrong. I am old enough to remember when in many parts of this country African Americans could not sit in the front of the bus: it was not *tolerated.* If, arguably, we are so politically correct today that we worry beyond reason about offending anyone, developing endless circumlocutions (e.g., "hearing impaired") for perfectly good expressions (e.g., "deaf"), the flip side is that it is a relief to observe that words like "chink," "spic," "wop," and "gook" have been thinned out. Prejudice never entirely disappears, of course, and we are wise to heed ongoing warnings against it.[18] Now, however, the warnings against such stereotypical prejudice are delivered with such massive condescension, and across so many arenas, that new forms of prejudice spring up like dandelions in a wild field. It is what James Kalb nicely calls "inquisitorial tolerance."[19] Bernard Goldberg puts the problem bluntly:

> Here's the problem, as far as I'm concerned: Over the years, as we became less closed-minded and more tolerant of all the right

18. Cf. Sandra L. Barnes, *Subverting the Power of Prejudice: Resources for Individual and Social Change* (Downers Grove: InterVarsity, 2006).

19. James Kalb, *The Tyranny of Liberalism: Understanding and Overcoming Administered Freedom, Inquisitorial Tolerance, and Equality by Command* (Wilmington: ISI Books, 2008).

things, like civil rights, somehow, we became *indiscriminately* tolerant. *"You're so judgmental"* became a major-league put-down in Anything Goes America — as if being judgmental of crap in the culture is a bad thing.[20]

Before probing these matters more deeply, it is worth reminding ourselves how widespread the problem is (chap. 2) and reflecting a little on the checkered history of tolerance (chap. 3).

---

20. Bernard Goldberg, *100 People Who Are Screwing Up America* (New York: HarperCollins, 2005), viii.

TWO

What Is Going On?

—⟊⟊⟊—

It doesn't take much trolling on the Internet to uncover some remarkably awful statements from the religious right:

> You say you're supposed to be nice to the Episcopalians and the Presbyterians and the Methodists and this, that, and the other thing. Nonsense. I don't have to be nice to the spirit of the Antichrist. I can love the people who hold false opinions but I don't have to be nice to them.[1]

> I want you to just let a wave of intolerance wash over you. I want you to let a wave of hatred wash over you. Yes, hate is good. . . . Our goal is a Christian nation. We have a Biblical duty, we are called by God, to conquer this country. We don't want equal time. We don't want pluralism.[2]

If this is one's only exposure to Christianity, one might easily develop a fair bit of sympathy for those on the left who find Christianity to be intolerant.

If Christian insiders were trying to read these two quotes as char-

---

1. Pat Robertson, *The 700 Club,* accessed 2 January 2010 at http://www.imdb.com/title/tt0149408/quotes.

2. Randall Terry, as reported in the *News Sentinel* of Fort Wayne, Indiana, for 16 August 1993.

itably as possible, they might point out that there is a species of sub-Christian scholarship that thinks Christian "love" seeks the other person's good in some sort of resolute fashion, without any necessary emotional component: you can love some nasty pervert, they might say, while emotionally hating their guts. The clause "hate is good" has a certain rationale to it: there is a biblical mandate to hate what is evil. Yet Christians at their best have known how to put together revulsion of godlessness with transparent love for people who are enemies, not least because they follow a Master who cried out in agony as he writhed on a cross, "Father, forgive them, for they do not know what they are doing" (Luke 23:34). If Christians speak of "conquering" a country by powerful evangelism, that is one thing; if they give the impression that they are going to impose their will on a nation by force of arms, or even by force of numbers, they are forgetting the distinctions the Bible itself makes between Christ and Caesar, between the church and the world, between legitimate expectations of what they think should take place now and what they hope will take place in the future. Worse, they also have an amazingly tin ear about how they are going to be heard outside their own circles.

Yet without justifying for a moment much of this rhetoric, Christians who take these stances do so *because they think the issues are of such importance they are worth contending for.* Most who respond to them do not engage with the issues the Christians want to raise, but simply outflank them by dismissing their intolerance with equal or greater intolerance.

As far back as 1991, the then-preeminent journalist Lance Morrow opened his essay in *Time* magazine's cover story "A Nation of Finger Pointers" with the following paragraphs:

> The busybody and the crybaby are getting to be the most conspicuous children on the American playground.
>
> The busybody is the bully with the ayatullah shine in his eyes, gauleiter of correctness, who barges around telling the other kids that they cannot smoke, be fat, drink booze, wear furs, eat meat or otherwise nonconform to the new tribal rules now taking shape.
>
> The crybaby, on the other hand, is the abject, manipulative little devil with the lawyer and, so to speak, the actionable diaper

rash. He is a mayor of Washington, arrested (and captured on videotape) as he smokes crack in a hotel room with a woman not his wife. He pronounces himself a victim — of the woman, of white injustice, of the universe. Whatever.

Both these types, the one overactive and the other overpassive, are fashioning some odd new malformations of American character. The busybodies have begun to infect the American society with a nasty *intolerance* [emphasis added] — a zeal to police the private lives of others and hammer them into standard forms. In Freudian terms the busybodies might be the superego of the American personality, the overbearing wardens. The crybabies are the messy id, all blubbering need and a virtually infantile irresponsibility.[3]

Add to this insightful and humorous analysis the fact that both the busybodies and the crybabies are accusing their opposite numbers of intolerance, and Morrow's piece remains a penetrating exposé of many of the polarizations that currently ravage public discourse. Irony is injected into the debate, however, when the intolerance of the busybodies is grounded, in their own minds, in their own tolerance — what Herbert Marcuse called "repressive tolerance."[4]

What I propose to do in this chapter is canvas some of the evidence from the past decade or so, beginning with a miscellany of examples, and then focusing more pointedly on examples in the domains of education, media, and sexual identity, ending with some observations on how much of this intolerant tolerance is fixated on opposing Christianity.

Miscellaneous Examples

In 2005, the Co-operative Bank, based in Manchester, England, asked a Christian organization, Christian Voice, to close its accounts at the Bank because its views were "incompatible" with the position of the

---

3. Lance Morrow, "A Nation of Finger Pointers," *Time,* 12 August 1991, 14. Cf. also http://www.time.com/time/printout/0,8816,973578,00.html.

4. For this reference I am indebted to James Bowman for his wonderfully insightful book, *Honor: A History* (New York: Encounter, 2006), 237.

Bank.[5] The public statement of the Bank reads as follows: "It has come to the bank's attention that Christian Voice is engaged in discriminatory pronouncements based on the grounds of sexual orientation. . . . This public stance is incompatible with the position of the Co-operative Bank, which publicly supports diversity and dignity in all its forms for our staff, customers and other stakeholders." Thus in the name of supporting diversity, the Bank eliminates one of its diverse customers! Even here it cannot be consistent: the Bank doubtless has Muslim customers who are no less willing than Christian Voice to condemn homosexual practice. After the BBC news report of the story was released, the Bank further stated: "We accept that everyone has the right to freedom of thought on religion; however, we do not believe that this entitles people to actively encourage and practice discrimination." Apparently the Bank thinks private religious thoughts are acceptable provided you do not act on them — which of course instantly trivializes religious belief. Meanwhile the word "discrimination" takes on the rhetorical power of "intolerance," without any rational reflection on the fact that most human beings discriminate a dozen times a day, and the entire culture is awash in discrimination: we do not hire pedophiles as school principals, we do not appoint a functional illiterate to head up NASA, and so forth. Indeed, the Bank itself has of course discriminated against Christian Voice. The issue ought to be whether any particular act of discrimination is good, sensible, and proper, for there are both good and evil forms of discrimination. But instead of engaging with the issue (in this case, homosexuality; Christian Voice had come to the attention of the Bank because it had publicly condemned plans to broadcast *Jerry Springer: The Opera,* describing it as blasphemous), the Co-operative Bank discriminated against Christian Voice on the grounds that Christian Voice discriminates against homosexuals.

In the autumn of 2007, Donald Hindley, a sociology professor at Brandeis University, lecturing on Latin American politics, told his students that Mexican immigrants to the U.S. used to be called

---

5. The matter received a great deal of public notice. The BBC account can be found at http://news.bbc.co.uk/2/hi/uk_news/4617849.stm (last accessed 2 January 2010).

"wetbacks." The bare fact cannot be contested. In fact, when in 1954 the Eisenhower administration attempted to repatriate more than a million illegal Mexicans, the official name of the project was Operation Wetback. In today's environment, however, a student complained. In the kerfuffle that followed, two students, apparently, said that Hindley's remarks were more than an explanation of a historical fact. At the time, Professor Hindley had been lecturing for forty-eight years with no previous recorded complaint. After prolonged administrative to-ing and fro-ing, the University found Hindley to be guilty of ethnic harassment and imposed a classroom monitor on him to ensure his speech was never out of line — all without granting him a formal hearing or putting the charges in writing before reaching the verdict. Unwilling to be labeled guilty of such harassment, Hindley has fought back. As of early 2010, the case had not been resolved, but the heated discussion has brought relations between faculty and administration to a tense standoff and prompted FIRE (= Foundation for Individual Rights in Education) to put Brandeis University on its list "as one of the worst abusers of liberty on campus."[6]

In the medical field, it is hard to remember that a few decades ago doctors took the Hippocratic Oath, which includes explicit clauses against taking life, understood to forbid both abortion and assisted suicide. Since then, almost all medical schools have dropped the Hippocratic Oath, or at the very least the offending clauses. The story, however, does not end there. Doctors, nurses, and other medical professionals who still want to live under the constraints of the Hippocratic Oath because of beliefs that prevent them from performing or participating in what are now legal but still ethically controversial acts find themselves in a strange situation. More and more pressure is being exerted on them either to act in violation of their consciences or to abandon medicine. Until recently, "conscience clauses" protected these medical professionals, permitting them to opt out of medical procedures contrary to their conscience. Now, however, various legislative proposals are attempting to eliminate such conscience clauses. Medical professionals who judge, say, abortion and assisted suicide to be immoral would have to violate their

6. http://www.thefire.org/case/755.html.

consciences or leave the profession. The most strident voices declare that doctors, pharmacists, nurses, and the rest must put patients' rights first. If they foresee that that could be problematic for them, they should choose another profession. Thus in the name of more tolerance for patients' rights, the rights of doctors and other medical professionals would be curtailed — even though those patients could always go to another doctor, and even though a bare four decades ago all doctors had to abide by the very ethic that the new tolerance wants to make illegal.

If present trends continue, the procedures at the center of this debate will go beyond abortion and assisted suicide. It is not unthinkable that medical practice will accommodate eugenic infanticide (already openly practiced in the Netherlands) and harvesting organs from patients with catastrophic cognitive impairment (long advocated in not a few medical journals). It is still uncertain how these matters will play out in court decisions.[7] My point is that the drive to enhance tolerance for diverse patients and their rights is demonstrably promoting intolerance to medical professionals.

The rising number of Muslims in England has prompted subtle (and not-so-subtle) eviction of pigs and their stories. In some schools, the story of the three little pigs is now banned, as Muslim school children might be offended by stories about unclean animals. The trend reached its silliest moment when the Council of Dudley, Worcestershire (West Midlands), banned all images or representations of pigs from its benefits department, on the ground that Muslims coming in for benefits might be offended. Calendars with pigs, porcelain porcine figurines, even pig-shaped stress relievers (spongy things you squeeze in your hand to relieve stress), all had to go, including a tissue box depicting Winnie the Pooh and Piglet — all this in a part of the country that traditionally has grown a lot of pigs. When pressed as to why pigs have to go, Mahbubur Rahman, a Muslim Councillor in West Midlands, explained, "It's a tolerance of people's beliefs." Stunning doublespeak! What about tolerance of those who think differently

---

7. The best brief suggestions as to what appropriate conscience clauses might look like are those of Wesley J. Smith, http://www.cbc-network.org/2009/05/protecting-the-careers-of-medical-professionals-who-believe-in-the-hippocratic-oath/, posted 27 May 2009.

about pigs? In the name of tolerance toward the beliefs of Muslims, intolerance is imposed. In this instance, as one media outlet has put it, "tolerance" has on the lips of Mahbubur Rahman and in the decisions of the Dudley Council become confused with "Islamist supremacism."[8] No one should doubt that Muslims ought to be free to express their dislike of pigs and pig representations; the problem, rather, is that Mr. Rahman thinks that getting rid of pigs and pig representations is a moral obligation that upholds the virtue of tolerance, whereas he senses himself under no obligation to uphold the virtue of tolerance and permit those who rather like pigs and their representations to keep them. Multiply this sort of confrontation a hundred times, and throw in a small but significant number of vociferous jihadist imams, and one understands why Prime Minister Cameron is at least raising some questions about how British immigration policy should be reviewed, not least to preserve a fundamentally tolerant (in the first sense) culture.

Or visit the website of the Harvard Chaplains.[9] Not all religious groups join the United Ministry organized by the Harvard Chaplains, so the Chaplains feel it necessary to warn against "certain destructive religious groups" who are not part of the United Ministry. The Chaplains "are committed to mutual respect and non-proselytization. We affirm the roles of personal freedom, doubt, and open critical reflection in healthy spiritual growth. . . . We're here to help you have a healthy, happy experience of your own spiritual journey while you're here at Harvard." I wonder if they think that's why Jesus came: to help us have a healthy, happy experience on our own spiritual journey. Meanwhile the Chaplains warn against, among other things, those who claim "a special relationship to God," and especially anything that qualifies as "ego destruction, mind control, manipulation of a member's relationships with family and friends."

On the editorial page of the *New York Times* for 24 November 2004, Nicholas D. Kristof writes a stinging attack on the "Left Behind" series written by Tim LaHaye and Jerry Jenkins, on the ground that these novels "enthusiastically depict Jesus returning to slaughter ev-

---

8. http://97.74.65.51/readArticle.aspx?ARTID=7048.
9. In particular, http://chaplains.harvard.edu/about_us.php.

eryone who is not a born-again Christian." Kristof accepts "that Mr. Jenkins and Mr. LaHaye are sincere," but then again so are Muslim fundamentalists. He adds, "Now, I've often written that blue staters should be less snooty toward fundamentalist Christians, and I realize that this column will seem pretty snooty. But if I praise the good work of evangelicals — like their superb relief efforts in Darfur — I'll also condemn what I perceive as bigotry." He then goes on to talk about the money the series is earning, impugning the motives of the authors, while poking fun (with not a little justification) at previous efforts in date-setting.

I suppose it is too much to hope that Kristof would distinguish between divergent Christian understandings of what takes place at the end. Christians who do not accept all the interpretations advanced by LaHaye and Jenkins, however, cannot hide behind these divergences, for the Bible itself not only mandates Christians to alleviate suffering (hence the kind of service in Darfur to which Kristof alludes) *but also contains a broad swath of exclusivism in which judgment by God is finally poured out on unbelievers.* Kristof, however, does not wrestle with how such teachings in the Bible might be integrated with everything else the Bible says, or with whether what it says might be true, or how every position, including his own, is making a truth claim that excludes other truth claims. He simply condemns what he does not like as bigotry.

Michel Houellebecq is one of France's most respected (if least comfortable) contemporary writers, with a sheaf of literary awards to his credit. His tone is that of a younger Albert Camus. In 2002 he was taken to court by four leading Muslim bodies in France. The charge was "making a racial insult" and "inciting religious hatred." This arose because in a magazine interview he made some derogatory comments about Islam. He dismissed Islam as "the dumbest religion" and unfavorably compared the Qur'an with the Bible: the former, he said, is poorly written, while the Bible "at least is beautifully written because the Jews have a heck of a literary talent." In the court case that followed, several prominent French intellectuals defended Houellebecq, but not a few sided with his accusers. The influential Human Rights League accused him of Islamophobia; many leftist writers insisted he was so vulgar he was not worth defending. But perhaps the most astute comments came from Salman Rushdie (who knows something of what it means to arouse Islamic ire), writing in the *Guardian:*

> But if an individual in a free society no longer has the right to say openly that he prefers one book to another, then that society no longer has the right to call itself free. Presumably any Muslim who said the Koran was much better than the Bible would then also be guilty of an insult, and absurdity would rule.
>
> As to "the dumbest religion," well, it's a point of view. And Houellebecq, in court, made the simple but essential point that to attack people's ideologies or belief-systems is not to attack the people themselves. This is surely one of the foundation principles of an open society. Citizens have the right to complain about discrimination against themselves, but not about dissent, even strongly worded, impolite dissent, from their thoughts. There cannot be fences erected around ideas, philosophies, attitudes or beliefs.[10]

Mercifully, the French court found in favor of the defendant.

In 2006, the wind ensemble of the Henry M. Jackson High School in Mill Creek, Washington, in line with its tradition of choosing a piece of music to play at graduation, voted unanimously for Franz Biebl's *Ave Maria.* The ensemble had played it for their winter concert and wanted to play it for graduation as well. The district superintendent, Carol Whitehead, turned it down: winter concerts were one thing, but to play the piece at graduation might be construed as endorsing religion. One student, Kathryn Nurre, sued, insisting that her constitutional rights had been violated. To read the letters to the editor in the *Seattle Times* is to gain an education on how tolerance so easily becomes intolerance. One writer applauded Whitehead for her decision, "for correctly insisting the wind ensemble play a more secular piece for commencement." After all, the "melody is very familiar to all of us [one suspects the writer is thinking of a different piece with the same title, but we'll let that pass], and when we hear the instruments play, the words are immediately heard

---

10. http://www.guardian.co.uk/books/2002/sep/28/fiction.michelhouellebecq.

in our brains."[11] As Jay Nordlinger comments, "Now we are in the vicinity of thought-crime: We may not be singing about God, and we may not be hearing words about God, but the notes make us think of God, which is verboten at graduation."[12] In *Nurre v. Whitehead,* the federal district court in Seattle ruled against the student. The case was appealed to the Ninth Circuit Court of Appeals, which upheld the ruling against the student. On 22 March 2010, the Supreme Court declined to hear a further appeal, which effectively left standing the decision of the Ninth Circuit, against the student.

Four years after thirteen people were shot and killed at Columbine High School, the school won its struggle to ban religious messages in its remembrance display. The father of victim Daniel Rohrbough wanted to include words that reflected his faith in the wake of this monumental tragedy; the school forbade it. The case worked its way up through the courts; the Supreme Court refused to hear it, so the decision of a lower court stands: the school won, and so did intolerance. The remembrance display must not include anything that suggests remembrance in ways that this particular family found most meaningful and helpful to them.

Enough. I could add many scores of examples, but you get the idea. In the name of not offending anyone, we are in danger of appealing to the virtue of tolerance to become more intolerant. It may be helpful to demonstrate how common this is in particular domains.

The Domain of Education

Here it might be useful to distinguish between what is going on in the broader academic world and what is transpiring in Christian colleges, seminaries, and universities.

In the former, it is easy to chart the rising pressure to conform to the new tolerance. Take the case of Scott McConnell, a graduate student in education at Le Moyne College. In 2005 he wrote a term paper

11. http://community.seattletimes.nwsource.com/archive/?date=20060705&slug=wedlets05.

12. "An Unpretty Pass: What a Song without Words Says about American Life," *National Review* 61, no. 20 (2 November 2009): 33.

arguing that the ideal classroom environment would be "based upon strong discipline and hard work" that could include "corporal punishment." He received an A- for his paper, in line with his 3.78 GPA. Some months later, however, he was dismissed from the College by the chair of the education department. She cited a "mismatch between [his] personal beliefs regarding teaching and learning and the Le Moyne College program goals." With the help of the Foundation for Individual Rights in Education (FIRE) and the Center for Individual Rights (CIR), McConnell took Le Moyne to court and won: he was reinstated into the program. He argued that the College had acted in bad faith: they had promised freedom of expression and then expelled him when he expressed himself.

Also in 2005, Noah Riner, then president of the Dartmouth Student Assembly, spoke at a convocation welcoming freshmen to the campus — a traditional responsibility of the student body president. He said that the acquisition of knowledge is less than what they should be striving for; the development of character is a more important goal. Then he added, "Character has a lot to do with sacrifice, laying our personal interests down for something bigger. The best example of this is Jesus. . . . He knew the right thing to do. He knew the cost would be agonizing torture and death. He did it anyway. That's character."[13] Noah Riner went on to talk briefly about what Jesus achieved on the cross.

Inevitably a controversy erupted. On the one hand, a vice president of the student body wrote to Riner, "I consider your choice of topic for the convocation speech reprehensible and an abuse of power. You embarrass the organization, you embarrass yourself." On the other, a Jewish student wrote, "Many of us in the Dartmouth community proudly disagree with that and other aspects of Riner's religious beliefs, but our disagreements do not give us the right to limit his speech."[14] One of the most insightful reflections on the brouhaha came from Noah Riner himself: "The problem is not that Dartmouth has a formalized speech code. That would be easy to deal with, and easy for students to break. The problem is that Dartmouth has a speech culture, where some topics are off limits and some perspec-

13. http://www.dartmouth.edu/news/releases/2005/09/20c.html.
14. http://dartreview.blogspot.com/2005_09_01_archive.html.

tives shouldn't be uttered." In other words, in this tolerant world some things are intolerable — especially those judged to be intolerant. Dartmouth College, of course, is the same institution which, several years earlier, forbade Campus Crusade from distributing one thousand copies of C. S. Lewis's *Mere Christianity* on the grounds that it might offend non-Christian students. Note well: the banned publication was not pornography, instructions on how to make a bomb, a book on pedophilia, or lessons on anarchy. Would Dartmouth have banned any such volumes on the ground that certain students might be offended? This book was a rather mild Christian apologetic first delivered as lectures on British radio during World War II. Vigorous protests eventually forced Dartmouth to reverse its decision.

Indeed, during the last ten years there have been attempts to "derecognize" chapters of InterVarsity Christian Fellowship (IVCF) at Tufts, Harvard, Rutgers, the University of North Carolina, and elsewhere. In each case, the local chapter was charged with being discriminatory, either because it insisted that its officers (though not its members) must subscribe to its statement of faith, or because it refused to accept among its officers those who advocated or practiced homosexuality. Thus the Undergraduate Council (or whatever body was involved in any specific case) discriminated against Christians on the ground that these Christians were discriminating against others. Usually there was little if any recognition on the part of the authorities that their zeal for non-discrimination was not only ironically inconsistent but was leading them into the specific form of discrimination forbidden by the First Amendment. So far, when these cases have been settled in court, the settlement has been in favor of the Christian organization.

Not so in the Hastings College of Law in the University of California. There the local chapter of the Christian Legal Society (CLS) was banned by the College on the ground that the chapter is discriminatory: it allowed only those who agree with the CLS statement of faith to fill leadership positions. In particular, Hastings asserted that CLS cannot require that its leaders, on the basis of the statement of faith, pledge to abstain from "unrepentant participation in or advocacy of a sexually immoral lifestyle." The lawsuit that followed wound its way up to the Supreme Court, which on a 5-4 vote ruled in favor of Hastings. Because the ruling comes from the highest court in the land, some see this decision as a harbinger of what will come: every evangelical group that takes a moral stand on U.S. campuses will be banned. The groups would continue, of course, off campus if necessary, in the catacombs as it were. Frankly, however, many legal experts do not expect that these nightmare scenarios will unfold: the ruling is narrow, and another case could be taken all the way to the Supreme Court if it could be shown that the policy is allowing infiltration of the group for subversive purposes, or if a similar ruling were *not* reached regarding, say, the requirements that a campus Muslim group might place on its leadership. Time will tell.

These struggles between Christian groups and universities have not been restricted to the United States.[15] In Britain, for instance, the same decade witnessed attempts by Birmingham University, Hull University, the University of Edinburgh, and two or three others to ban the local Christian Union (CU — a local chapter of Universities and Colleges Christian Fellowship [UCCF], the British equivalent of American IVCF) from their campuses for very similar reasons. Although these challenges sometimes go on for two or three years, so far they have had a happy result. What is so interesting, however, is the way in which universities, historically the bastions of free speech and free thinking, have repeatedly, in the name of tolerance, exhibited remarkable intolerance. In the case of Edinburgh University, for instance, the authorities banned the CU from meeting on campus to discuss sexual ethics, on the ground that the orthodox Christian view is offensive to homosexuals. In one case the situation became so ludicrous that even the liberal newspaper the *Guardian* became sympathetic to the CU, opening its editorial pages to an essay by Richard Cunningham, the Director of UCCF. Cunningham wrote, "GK Chesterton once said that, 'The purpose of an open mind is the same as that of an open mouth — to close it again on something solid.' If 'open mindedness' is being defined as a refusal to make judgements about religious truth and sexual ethics (for instance) then we are prone to contracting a form of intellectual lock jaw."[16]

---

15. I discussed some of the reasons for the diverse patterns in *Christ and Culture Revisited* (Grand Rapids: Eerdmans, 2008), 186-90.

16. http://www.guardian.co.uk/education/2006/nov/28/highereducation.students.

Not all of this academic passion for the new tolerance is directed against Christians, of course. In 2006, Bob Averill, a student at the Art Institute of Portland, Oregon, and a committed atheist (he even ran a blog called *Portland Atheist*), walked up to an informal group of students who, after class, were discussing spirituality. Averill challenged one particular student's religious beliefs. He did not question her right to hold them, but asked, rather, what evidence she had to back them up. The nature of these beliefs? She believed in astral projections and leprechauns living on another energy level. The student complained to the authorities, and after several rounds in which Averill's exchange with the other student was described as an "altercation" and his attempt to bring in another student who had witnessed the exchange was taken as "rude and belligerent behavior," Averill was dismissed from the Institute with less than a year to go before graduation.[17] For its part, the Institute claimed it dismissed Averill on the ground that his behavior was "aggressive, demeaning, and threatening."[18]

Nor are these pressures restricted to students. On 15 September 2004, a longtime adjunct professor at DePaul University, Thomas Klocek, observed a pair of tables set up by student activists. Those activists represented two groups, Students for Justice in Palestine (SJP) and United Muslims Moving Ahead (UMMA). He engaged the students on their claims, pointing out that historically the term "Palestinian" is problematic because it was once a generic term that referred to Muslims, Jews, and Christians who lived in a geographical area rather than to a single ethnicity. One of the students said she was deeply insulted by his remarks. Inevitably the discussion was ratcheted up until the students claimed the Israelis are treating the Palestinians the way Hitler treated the Jews. Klocek argued that there are some important differences. What happened next is disputed. Klocek claims he realized that discussion was futile, put down the flyer calmly, and thumbed his chin, Italian-style, to indicate "I'm outta here!" The students claimed he threw his flyer onto the table and gave them the finger. The entire encounter lasted about fifteen

---

17. http://www.portlandmercury.com/portland/Content?oid=84436&category=22101.

18. http://chronicle.com/article/For-Profit-College-Says-It/37892.

minutes. Despite the fact that he had an enviable record of teaching, Klocek was promptly suspended. He took the case to court, suing DePaul for defamation. After four years (!), Cook County Circuit Court Judge Charles Winkler dismissed the case (March 2009). Klocek appealed; at this writing, the case has not yet been decided.[19] Regardless of the rights and wrongs of particular arguments, it is difficult to avoid the conclusion that DePaul University destroyed Klocek's academic career to placate a group of students who could not tolerate an opinion counter to their own without complaining they were insulted and demeaned — and the cultural assumption of the new tolerance tends to work in their favor in the adjudication process. In his important 2005 essay, John J. Miller details many instances of professors in America who have faced similar challenges.[20]

In one sense, of course, the spirit of tolerance on college and university campuses can be a helpful thing: it is sometimes easier for a Christian to find a place at the table today than it was thirty or forty years ago. But the price is high: if the Christian maintains that there is an exclusive element in Christian confessionalism, which of course implies that others are in some measure wrong, the place at the table is often quickly withdrawn. The grounds for the withdrawal are not, formally speaking, that the Christian is a Christian, but that the Christian is intolerant, which cannot be tolerated. Thus the world of academia exerts not-so-subtle pressures for Christians to develop a form of (ostensibly) Christian expression that disowns or at least silences the exclusiveness claims that are grounded in Scripture itself. As Nathan Hatch puts it:

> The modern intellectual world is adrift, incapable or unwilling to allow any claim of certainty to set the coordinates by which ideas and commitments are to be judged. The positive side of this situation, of course, is that toleration and subjectivity have become the

19. http://illinoisreview.typepad.com/illinoisreview/2009/04/judge-throws-out-thomas-klocek-case-against-depaulappeal-planned-.html.
20. "Pariahs, Martyrs — and Fighters Back: Conservative Professors in America," *National Review* 57, no. 19 (2005): 40-45. It should be pointed out that some of the professors Miller surveys are not all that conservative: Klocek, for instance, voted Democrat.

principal virtues of our age, meaning that marginal groups —
even evangelicals — are accorded far more respect than they were
earlier in the century. The danger . . . is that the gentle lamb of toleration often returns as the wolf of relativism. Christians, then,
are both better off and worse off: better in that they are tolerated
like everyone else, worse in that no claim to truth carries weight
any longer.[21]

If these are the things that are going on in the broader academic
world, what is transpiring in Christian tertiary institutions?

Like children long rejected, evangelical scholars are still too anx-
ious to be accepted by their peers, too willing to move only in di-
rections that allow them to be "relevant." [The result is that] we
have been far more inclined to speak up when our Christian convictions are in tune with the assumptions of modern academic life
than when they are at odds. It is much easier, for instance, to set
oneself in the vanguard of social progress than it is to defend
those Christian assumptions that the established and fashionable intellectual circles of our day regard as obscurantist and fan-
ciful. Yet it is this tougher mental fight that we must not avoid.[22]

These pressures must be faced not only when the Christian academic
operates in, say, a state university, but even when he or she is en-
sconced in a Christian college. The uniqueness of Christ, Trinitarian
theology, the claims of what was achieved exclusively by Jesus' death
and resurrection, the insistence that the God of the Bible is the Creator and Judge of all — "these claims are intolerable, and Christians
will be constantly pressured, both directly and indirectly, to tone
them down. If we do not, there will be a price to pay, in reputation or
prestige if no other. No matter how winsomely we manage to handle
ourselves, if we in Christian higher education are determined to live

---

21. Nathan O. Hatch, "Evangelical Colleges and the Challenge of Christian
Thinking," in *Making Higher Education Christian: The History and Mission of Evangelical
Colleges in America,* ed. Joel A. Carpenter and Kenneth W. Shipps (Grand Rapids: Chris-
tian University Press, 1987), 163.

22. Hatch, "Evangelical Colleges and the Challenge of Christian Thinking," 166-
67.

out our allegiance to Christ we will, as Jesus himself instructs us, experience some of his reproach."[23]

Genuine pluralism within the broader culture is facilitated when there is a strong Christian voice loyal to the Scriptures — as well as strong Muslim voices, skeptical voices, Buddhist voices, atheistic voices, and so forth. Genuine pluralism within the broader culture is *not* fostered when in the name of tolerance none of the voices can say that any of the others is wrong, and when this stance is the only ultimate virtue.

The Domain of the Media

Louis Bolce and Gerald De Maio conducted a Lexis-Nexis database search of how three newspapers, the *New York Times, Los Angeles Times,* and *Washington Post,* wrote about the culture wars during the decade 1990-2000. During that span of time, these three papers published only eighteen articles "linking the culture wars to the secularist-religious cleavage dividing the Democratic and Republican parties."[24] During the same span, they published fifty-nine stories about the role played by secularists in these conflicts, along with a whopping 929 articles about the political machinations of evangelical and fundamentalist Christians. In other words, in the media perception, the divergences developing in the country are regularly laid at the door of those who are *not* well-represented in the media.

Because the new tolerance, an ostensibly value-free tolerance, has become the dominant religion among media leaders, this vision is constantly reinforced. For instance, the media may present popes such as John Paul II and Benedict XVI in a positive light, provided these popes are restricting themselves to ceremony or world poverty, but if they show how their beliefs impinge on social issues such as premarital and extramarital sex, abortion, homosexuality, and euthanasia, then they must be bigoted, out of date, slightly bizarre, even dangerous, and certainly intolerant.

23. Duane Litfin, *Conceiving the Christian College* (Grand Rapids: Eerdmans, 2004), 81-82.

24. "The Politics of Partisan Neutrality," *National Review* 143 (May 2004): 9.

In 2001, former CBS newsman Bernard Goldberg published a book with the title *Bias: A CBS Insider Exposes How the Media Distort the News*.[25] His thesis is not that the media are controlled by a liberal versus conservative bias per se, nor by a Democrat versus Republican bias. Rather, their bias is generated by a kind of social, cultural, intellectual, and professional inbreeding. They think of themselves as wonderfully diverse and broadly representative of the nation because they make sure they hire a representative mix of gender and race. What is lacking, however, is a representative mix of intellectual and cultural positions; there is little diversity of thought. The media will display a deep and thoughtful commitment to ensuring they have a representative number of women on board, but these women — and men — will not hold representative views on abortion, gun control, homosexuality, and the importance of religion in one's life. Thus, while they feel they are on the cutting edge of a profound tolerance, there are many domains of the media's life that are hugely intolerant. Inevitably, even while hardworking journalists are doing their best to be responsible and as objective as possible, the common narrowness of these horizons fosters patterns of distortion in the news that become troubling.[26]

This has been going on for decades. In 1972, Pauline Kael, movie critic for the *New Yorker,* won a bit of immortality for herself by announcing, after the elections that returned Nixon to power, "I can't believe it! I don't know a single person who voted for him." Considering Nixon won forty-nine of the fifty states, Kael managed to do nothing more than demonstrate her rather sad isolation from most people in the nation.

The Domain of Homosexual Behavior

For more than two decades, the Boy Scouts of America have been under attack for (a) not admitting girls; (b) not admitting atheists; and

---

25. Washington: Regnery, 2001.

26. Cf. L. Brent Bozell III and Brent H. Baker, ed., *And That's the Way It Isn't: A Reference Guide to Media Bias* (Alexandria: Media Research Center, 1990).

(c) not permitting avowed homosexuals to serve in any leadership capacity. After numerous expensive lawsuits, the Boy Scouts thought they had secured some tranquility when in 2000 the Supreme Court's *Dale* decision ruled that as a private organization the Boy Scouts were entitled to choose their own members. But although the ACLU (= American Civil Liberties Union) lost in that ruling, it did not give up. Instead, it has joined with assorted gay-rights groups to attack the Boy Scouts' ties to public institutions, which are numerous and complicated. For instance, the Scouts often recruit in public schools and are given special treatment in the use of state and national parks for their jamborees. On the other hand, these privileges are in one sense paid for. In the summer of 2008, for instance, the Order of the Arrow organized "Five Sites, Five Weeks, Five Thousand Arrowmen," a project in which five thousand volunteers devoted five weeks to assorted conservation projects and improving of public facilities in national forests across the country. Since 2004, the Boy Scouts have devoted something close to ten million hours in assisting public programs and improving public property. Another project of the Boy Scouts, "Good Turn for America," cleans up hundreds of city parks and schoolyards. To become an Eagle Scout, a candidate must lead his troop in a community service project. Scouts in Arizona have invested thousands of hours in fire prevention and conservation projects in and around the Grand Canyon.

So the ACLU and others have pounced on the Scouts in numerous struggles, none directly related to homosexuality, all having to do with the relationship of the Scouts to public land and public institutions. In 2003, the ACLU, on behalf of a lesbian couple and an agnostic couple, argued that the Scouts are a religious organization and therefore its leases with San Diego violate the establishment clause. These leases have enabled the Scouts to run Camp Balboa and a half-acre on Fiesta Island for almost a century, during which time they have spent millions of their own dollars to develop the properties, keeping them open to the public. The resulting lawsuits continue.

In 1928, Philadelphia leased a half-acre of property to the Scouts, and they in turn constructed a 7,500-square-foot Beaux Arts headquarters at their own expense. In 2000, the Philadelphia city council tried to evict the Scouts, and when that demand failed, demanded $200,000 per annum in rent. The Scouts must pay up or stop discriminating against homosexuals and atheists. Quite apart from questions of equity — who really owns that building in which none of the money invested came from the city? — would it not be more pluralistic and genuinely tolerant for the city to say that if homosexuals and/or atheists want to build a similar institution, the city of Philadelphia will be just as helpful to them as they have been in the past to the Scouts? No, that will never do: what the new tolerance *means* is that government must be intolerant of those who do not accept the new definition of tolerance. These two locations, San Diego and Philadelphia, stand for numerous other struggles the Scouts have endured during the past decade, mostly on the coasts, all in the name of tolerance.

It is not easy to predict how these and similar cases will turn out. Two years ago in Massachusetts, Catholic Charities was told it had to withdraw from its adoption service or change its policies and become willing to place children with same-sex couples. Catholic Charities stopped its service. How this will benefit needy children in that state is less than clear. One might argue that Catholic Charities could have and should have put up a better fight. World Vision, an evangelical charity, requires that its employees refrain from extramarital sexual activity, including, of course, homosexual activity. In 2005, World Vision was awarded $1.5 million by the Office of Justice Programs to address escalating juvenile and gang violence in Virginia. Eventually lawyers were called in to determine if World Vision was discriminatory. The Department of Justice eventually (2007) ruled in favor of World Vision on the basis of the Religious Freedom Restoration Act (RFRA) of 1993. After all, as Carl Esbeck, a law professor at the University of Missouri, observes, "[N]onreligious organizations receiving federal grant monies freely hire based on their core mission, just as Planned Parenthood requires that employees be pro-choice and Sierra Club screens applicants based on their view of global warming. Religious groups likewise cannot remain true to their founding creedal purposes unless employees are aligned with the energizing core of the mission."[27] Indeed, Esbeck goes on to say, "One who has never disagreed with others about religion is not thereby commendably tolerant, but is treating re-

27. http://library.findlaw.com/2008/Jun/1/247208.html.

ligious differences as trivial, as if religious beliefs do not matter. That is just a soft form of religious bigotry."[28]

Sometimes common sense prevails.

And sometimes it doesn't. "On June 29, 2004, Pastor Ake Green was sentenced to one month in jail for showing 'disrespect' against homosexuals in the sermon he delivered from his pulpit in the small town of Borgholm, Sweden on July 20, 2003."[29] In 2008, the Supreme Court of California ruled that two physicians could not legally refuse artificial insemination to a woman because she is a lesbian. The doctors had not withheld the service because they disagreed with her: they argued that they happily provide medical care to all kinds of people with whom they disagree. They would not withhold cancer treatment from a rapist, for example. But where they felt they had to draw a line was in their own participation in an act that they judged to be immoral. It was not as if the patient, Guadalupe Benitez, could not obtain the services elsewhere; the lawsuit was not about being unable to obtain the medical services she desired, but about making a point. In its decision, the Court stated, "Do the rights of religious freedom and free speech, as guaranteed in both the federal and the California Constitutions, exempt a medical clinic's physicians from complying with the California Unruh Civil Rights Act's prohibition against discrimination based on a person's sexual orientation? Our answer is no."[30]

The wording is important. If homosexuality is made an *exclusively* civil rights issue, then courts will be tempted to limit First Amendment rights time and again. The issue is becoming complicated. Elane Photography, a business owned by an evangelical husband-and-wife team, refused to photograph the gay commitment ceremony of two women. In 2006, Vanessa Willcock filed a complaint with the New Mexico Human Rights Commission, which eventually found against Elane Photography and ordered it to pay $6,637 for Willcock's legal fees. The decision was appealed to the District Court, where once again Elane Photography lost (December 2009). Elane

28. http://library.findlaw.com/2008/Jun/1/247208.html.
29. http://www.akegreen.org.
30. The case has been reported in many places. See, for instance, http://www.spectrummagazine.org/node/1200.

Photography is appealing: if business owners are forced to do something against their own conscience, such as a photography company owned and operated by deeply committed vegetarians being forced to photograph the slaughter of animals and the preparation of meat for a butcher shop, where is the tolerance and equity in that?[31] Outside the U.S., nations ostensibly in favor of human rights are becoming increasingly restrictive. In England, a Catholic school was recently forbidden to fire its openly gay headmaster. Parochial (Anglican) schools are forbidden to teach that homosexuality is sin. In Canada, the Alberta Human Rights Commission forbade a Christian pastor from making "disparaging" remarks about homosexuality, or even repeating biblical condemnations.

In the past, there has been no shortage of cruel and contemptible things said about and to homosexuals by conservatives. But it seems to many of us that unrestrained venom now more characteristically flows in the opposite direction. When she was still Miss California, Carrie Prejean was asked what she thought of gay marriage. She replied that "marriage should be between a man and a woman. No offense to anybody out there, but that's how I was raised." She did not turn out to be the best defender of the traditional view, but her language was mild compared with what was thrown back at her. "A dumb bitch with half a brain," opined Perez Hilton, a gay columnist. "An ignorant disgrace" who "makes me sick to my stomach," writes Giuliana Rancic, E! News anchor. This is the tolerance that is being commended?

Target: Christianity

At the risk of sounding paranoid or petty, I must say that a disproportionate part of the intolerance that masks itself as (the new) tolerance is directed against Christians and Christianity.

Public libraries have been known to ban a book such as John

---

31. http://speakupmovement.wordpress.com/2009/12/16/elane-photography-plans-appeal-of-negative-ruling-by-new-mexico-court/. For some of the complexities of the issue, see http://volokh.com/tag/elane-photography-v-willock/.

MacArthur's *Safe in the Arms of God.*[32] In several countries — Australia, Canada, the United Kingdom — legislation has been passed that has resulted in Christian pastors being hauled before the courts, and sometimes found guilty of hate crimes, on the ground that they have given public addresses that contrasted Christianity and Islam in ways that were judged to vilify Islam. I know of no instance in these countries where similar charges were brought against an imam for comparisons running in the opposite direction.

In 2004, in the Russian city of Beslan, Islamic terrorists took 1,200 people hostage in a public school. They ultimately slaughtered 344 people, 186 of them students. On a smaller scale, but still horrific, two disturbed students massacred thirteen people at Columbine High School. In the wake of such events, it is not surprising that many schools have run drills so that teachers and students alike will have some idea how to react if such violence breaks out in their schools — locking classroom doors, staying below window level, and so forth, while coordinating the work of police and other public safety officials. In New Jersey in April 2007, one such drill was run by the Burlington Police Department. And who were the mock terrorists supposed to be? Homeschooling Christian fundamentalists. Three years earlier, a similar drill in Muskegon County, Michigan, featured homeschooling wackos who detonate a bomb on a school bus.

Some local exasperation followed. But can you imagine what would have happened if the mock terrorists had been depicted as turban-wearing Islamic jihadists? Can one think of a single instance of organized Christian homeschoolers threatening, let alone carrying out, terrorist violence?

I have already listed a handful of instances of intolerance in colleges and universities. Of course, anecdotal evidence by itself does not demonstrate a trend. One or two recent essays, however, in addition to providing many more examples, document case after case of astonishing intolerance *where the only common ingredient was that the student or faculty member in question was a Christian.*[33] Scott Savage

---

32. http://rabbiphilosopher.blogspot.com/2006/10/banned-books-john-mcarthur.html.

33. See the important essay by David French, "Expelling God from the University," *Academic Questions* 19 (2006): 75-84. The examples that follow are drawn from his essay.

volunteered to serve on a book selection committee that recommended books for freshmen. Others on the committee listed a number of books from a leftist perspective; Savage, a quiet pacifist, suggested several conservative volumes, including David Kupelian's *The Marketing of Evil,* which refers to homosexual behavior as sinful or evil. Some homosexual faculty complained that this book recommendation made them feel "unsafe" on the campus, and so the faculty voted, without dissent, to accuse the student of sexual harassment. Emily Brooker saw no problem in exploring alternative views on sexual and family matters in the classroom, but refused to sign a joint letter whose purpose was to support same-sex "family" adoption. For this stance she was investigated by the social work department and charged with ethics violations. A professor of English literature at Sonoma State University, lecturing on James Joyce, drew a picture of two mountains on the board at the front of the class, stated that Joyce's ecclesiastical background taught him that the one mountain represented God and the other represented human beings, and the only way between the two — here he drew a cross in the valley, touching both peaks — was Christ on the cross, connecting people with God. He then broke into peals of laughter, drawing the class into the humor.

Quite apart from the fact that this is not a good way to teach English literature,[34] can one imagine getting away with this if the derision had been directed against Buddhism or Islam? Or against Muhammad himself? Remember those Danish cartoons? In many circles it seems that the only broadly sanctioned derision still permitted is anti-Christian. In the nature of the case this derision is in support of what is widely perceived to be a more tolerant outlook.

It is not the derision that perplexes Christians. If they know their Bibles, they will not be too surprised (e.g., John 15:18-25). What surprises and perplexes Christians when they face this sort of opprobrium is that it is offered in defense of large-hearted "tolerance." In any society, various sectors criticize other sectors. The right criticizes

---

34. Contrast Daniel E. Ritchie, *Reconstructing Literature in an Ideological Age: A Biblical Poetics and Literary Studies from Milton to Burke* (Grand Rapids: Eerdmans, 1996).

the left, and the left criticizes the right.[35] None of that is troubling; in a liberal democracy, all of it is healthy. What is *un*healthy is derisive criticism that does not engage with the views of a particular party, but merely dismisses them and tries to expel them from the discourse *on the ground that they are intolerant.*[36]

As this book was being written, the remarkable responses to Brit Hume hit the press. He was asked on a Fox News panel what advice he would give to Tiger Woods in the wake of Tiger's tragic sex scandal. Among other things, Hume said, rather softly and gently:

> He's said to be a Buddhist. I don't think that faith offers the kind of forgiveness and redemption that is offered by the Christian faith. . . . My message to Tiger would be, "Tiger, turn to the Christian faith, and you can make a total recovery and be a great example to the world."[37]

The explosive reaction was predictable. Tom Shales, TV critic of the *Washington Post,* derisively mocked the notion that Christians should "run around trying to drum up new business." Hume "doesn't really have the authority, does he, unless one believes that every Christian by mandate must proselytize? . . . [T]he remark will probably rank . . . as one of the most ridiculous of the year"; he has "dissed about half a billion Buddhists on the planet." Keith Olbermann, formerly of MSNBC, declared that Hume had tried to "threaten Tiger Woods into becoming a Christian." David Shuster, Olbermann's colleague, charged that Hume had denigrated his own religion by bringing it up on a talk show, and found Hume's comments "truly embarrassing."

35. E.g., compare Randall Balmer, *Thy Kingdom Come: How the Religious Right Distorts the Faith and Threatens America: An Evangelical's Lament* (New York: Basic, 2006), and Newt Gingrich, *Rediscovering God in America: Reflections on the Role of Faith in Our Nation's History and Future* (Nashville: Integrity, 2006).

36. One thinks of the spate of remarkably inaccurate books: Chris Hedges, *American Fascists: The Christian Right and War on America* (New York: Free Press, 2007); Michelle Goldberg, *Kingdom Coming: The Rise of Christian Nationalism* (New York: Norton, 2006); James Rudin, *The Baptizing of America: The Religious Right's Plans for the Rest of Us* (New York: Thunder's Mouth, 2006). Cf. discussion in Carson, *Christ and Culture Revisited,* 183-85.

37. Both this and the subsequent quotations are easily found on multiple websites.

Blogger Andrew Sullivan called Hume's comments "pure sectarianism," an improper attempt to abolish "the distinction between secular and religious discourse."

The criticisms of Hume prompt a raft of reflections. (1) Factually, what Hume said about Buddhism was essentially correct. Every religion includes in its structure some understanding of what is "wrong" with human beings and presents a "solution." For Christianity, the root problem is sin — idolatrous defiance of the one Creator-God; the solution is forgiveness of sin, secured by Christ's death and resurrection. For Buddhism, the root problem is ignorance about the true nature of reality, in particular the impermanence of all things, an ignorance that results in craving and attachment; the solution therefore is enlightenment.[38] One may argue which of these two perceptions of reality, if either, is true. Hume's point, however, is this: he understands Tiger Woods to have committed sin, and what Tiger most needs is forgiveness, not least forgiveness by God, as part of the healing and transformation he hopes Tiger experiences. That is a Christian analysis, of course, but granted that this sort of forgiveness is what Tiger needs, Tiger is not going to find it in Buddhism, where the structure of thought is entirely different. There is no "sin" in Buddhism, as many religions conceive of "sin." Some thoughtful Buddhists replied by offering their alternative structure: that is fair dialog in a liberal democracy. And that is what was lacking from so many media pundits. (2) When the critics mock Hume for supposing he has a "mandate" to "proselytize," Christians quietly smile and remember the Great Commission. If by "proselytize" one means something like "try to win people to faith in Jesus by humble articulation of the gospel and without any external coercion," that is exactly the mandate that Christians have. (3) In the long haul, there can be no freedom of religion unless people of competing faiths and of no faith are free to proselytize, free to try to convince others. (4) In any case, isn't that exactly what Olbermann, Shuster, and Sullivan *et al.* are trying to do — convince people that *their* view of reality is correct? Thoughtful Christians will not want Olbermann, Shuster, and Sullivan to be silenced or

---

38. See, most recently, the careful book by Keith Yandell and Harold Netland, *Buddhism: A Christian Exploration and Appraisal* (Downers Grove: InterVarsity, 2009).

to withdraw from the marketplace of ideas; they merely note, with quiet irony, that the most intemperate language is being used by those calling for "tolerance." To accuse Hume of "dissing" Buddhism because he disagrees with it is to cast a rhetorical spin on Hume's comments — but fair-minded readers may be excused for thinking that Hume is being "dissed" rather more virulently. (5) Sullivan's charge that Hume has crossed the border between secular and religious discourse already presupposes (a) the intrinsic superiority of secular discourse and (b) that religious discourse is viable and respectable *only* when it is utterly private. But countless millions cannot agree with (a), and Sullivan presents no argument for justifying that stance: he merely presupposes it and tries to impose it on others. As for (b), the assumption that religion in general and Christianity in particular must be entirely privatized, that is something to be explored a little later in this book.

We ought to remind ourselves, however, of the way that liberal democracy is supposed to work. The price of citizenship in a liberal democracy is that citizens will not impose their convictions on others; they will not use the power of the state to coerce belief. Each person is free to practice his or her belief or unbelief. But as Ross Douthat rightly points out, "That's the theory. In practice, the admirable principle that nobody should be persecuted for their beliefs often blurs into the more illiberal idea that nobody should ever publicly criticize another religion. Or champion one's own faith as an alternative. Or say anything whatsoever about religion, outside the privacy of church, synagogue or home."[39] Of course, these illiberal notions have as much right to a hearing as does the Christianity of Brit Hume. But if those illiberal notions gain broad sway, they, and not Hume's Christianity, would be responsible for squashing pluralism.

This needs a little more unpacking. After the destruction of the World Trade Center, Andrew Sullivan wrote an article for the *New York Times Magazine* comparing Christian fundamentalists with Muslim terrorists on the ground that both hold to exclusivist beliefs.[40] But

39. http://www.nytimes.com/2010/01/11/opinion/11douthat.html.
40. "This *Is* a Religious War," *New York Times Magazine* (7 October 2001); available online at http://faculty.plts.edu/gpence/html/This%20is%20a%20Religious%20War.htm.

this analysis misconstrues both the nature of democracy and the locus of the real danger. The danger does not lie in tenaciously held exclusivist beliefs: compare the mutually exclusive economic analyses of Ronald Reagan and Barack Obama. Mutually exclusive beliefs, religious or otherwise, are not dangerous, provided there is also a mutual commitment to ongoing discourse, *to the older kind of tolerance.* As Duane Litfin puts it, "The danger, whether under religious auspices (the Inquisition, the Taliban) or secular (Nazism, Stalinism), stems from the totalitarian recourse to coercion. In this light, for Sullivan to equate the fundamentalism of a Jerry Falwell to that of Osama Bin Laden is both unfair and misguided."[41]

41. Litfin, *Conceiving the Christian College,* 265n.13.

THREE

Jottings on the History of Tolerance

—⟶⟶⟶—

Initial Comments to Orient the Discussion

Every culture and every age necessarily displays *some* tolerance and *some* intolerance. No culture can be tolerant of everything or intolerant of everything: it is simply not possible. A culture that tolerates, say, genocide (e.g., the Nazis) will not tolerate, say, the Jews it wants to kill or homosexual practice. A culture that tolerates just about every sexual liaison may nevertheless balk at, say, rape, or pedophilia, or in many cases bigamy and polygamy. If we are going to think carefully about tolerance and intolerance, a little historical perspective will help.[1] As the chapter title suggests, these are mere jottings, observations on certain movements and writers who have influenced discussion of tolerance across the centuries, including some contemporary thought on the matter.

---

1. This is one of the great merits of the work by Alexandra Walsham, *Charitable Hatred: Tolerance and Intolerance in England, 1500-1700* (Manchester: Manchester University Press, 2006). Many historians have unwisely pitted tolerance and intolerance against each other as mere polar opposites: if one wins, the other loses, and it is comfortable today to hold that tolerance is winning. The historical realities, not only in Walsham's period but in every period, are far more complex, not only because tolerance and intolerance are both *always* present in any culture in some form or other, but also because both tolerance and intolerance can, on some moral scales, be either a virtue or a vice, as we shall see.

47

Since we are casting an eye backward across the centuries, the tolerance of which I am now writing is of course what I have called the older tolerance. It is nicely defined by Edward Langerak:

> Toleration is the enduring of something disagreeable. Thus it is not indifference toward things that do not matter and it is not broad-minded celebration of differences. It involves a decision to forgo using powers of coercion, so it is not merely resignation at the inevitability of the disagreeable, although begrudging toleration can be granted when one believes that coercion, while possible, would come at too high a price. Tolerating another's actions is quite compatible with trying to change another's mind, as long as one relies on rational persuasion — or, perhaps, emotional appeals — rather than blunt threats or subtle brainwashing.
>
> Religious toleration generally applies to *expressing* or *acting upon* theologically-related beliefs, although the mere *holding* of beliefs or the *persons* holding them have also been the objects of intolerance and toleration. . . . [I]n spite of some behavioral similarities, toleration is distinct from the sort of pluralistic ecumenicism that seeks consensus on central religious matters or views other religious beliefs as simply different routes to similar goals. We can take religions extremely seriously, believe that we are clearly right and others are egregiously wrong on a matter of huge and holy significance, and still decide to tolerate their propagation of the error.[2]

It may be helpful to indicate briefly the direction that the historical jottings take in this chapter. These jottings are not merely random observations on what took place in the past; rather, they illustrate that across the ages the best thinking on the subject, however diverse, displays a remarkable connection between one's understanding of tolerance and one's understanding of "natural law" or "public moral law" (or whatever it is called in various contexts). Historical treatments that fail to probe this connection, however interesting their discrete observations, have wittingly or unwittingly elevated tolerance to the

---

2. Edward Langerak, "Theism and Toleration," in *A Companion to Philosophy of Religion,* ed. Philip L. Quinn and Charles Taliaferro (Oxford: Blackwell, 1997), 514.

place of supreme virtue, so that its relations with other virtues are largely obscured.[3] The result is that tolerance itself is distorted.

J. Daryl Charles rightly argues that in the pre-Christian Greco-Roman world, the line from Heraclitus (c. 535-475 B.C.) through Aristotle (384-322 B.C.) down to the Stoics embraced a form of what would later be called "natural law" theory — a vision of moral order based on human nature and the outworking of that nature in reason.[4] In the Christian heritage, the massive influence of Thomas Aquinas — whether within the Roman Catholic tradition and the articulation of natural law, or sometimes adapted, especially in the Reformed tradition, to speak of the *imago Dei* and the constraints of common grace — worked itself out in a variety of ethical structures that sought the common good in any culture. Within such large frameworks of moral reasoning, tolerance is seen as a virtue because of its concern for the common good. Once tolerance is cut loose from this larger moral vision, however, and becomes shackled to notions of individual freedom to do what one pleases absent much consideration of the common good, it becomes quite a different sort of beast. Charles might usefully devote more attention to the teaching of Jesus regarding the distinction between Christ and Caesar and the role that Jesus' teaching played in the development of tolerance in the West. (We will shortly have occasion to reflect on this theme.) Yet the tight connec-

3. E.g., Graham N. Stanton and Guy G. Stroumsa, *Tolerance and Intolerance in Early Judaism and Christianity* (Cambridge: Cambridge University Press, 1998), is made up of essays that usefully explore the patterns of tolerance and intolerance within various Jewish and Christian groups, but there is fairly little exploration of how such tolerance is located within a larger moral vision. The exception is that some of the contributors question whether tolerance is invariably a good thing, while others think that tolerance is rather sadly limited wherever there is a notion of *revealed* religion. Similarly, a contemporary reference work like that of H. Knox Thames, *International Religious Freedom Advocacy: A Guide to Organizations, Law, and NGOs* (Waco: Baylor University Press, 2009), is a wonderful resource that equips travelers, activists, assorted agencies, and others to become familiar with what is and is not being done to safeguard religious liberty, and what resources are available within the UN, the European Union, the Organization of American States, the African Union, and so on. But of course it is not the sort of book that reflects deeply on the nature of tolerance.

4. J. Daryl Charles, "Truth, Tolerance, and Christian Conviction: Reflections on a Perennial Question — a Review Essay," *Christian Scholar's Review* 36 (2007): esp. 201-11.

tion Charles maintains between tolerance and moral vision is not only historically important but also must play a major role in our assessment of what is happening today.

A. J. Conyers argues along similar lines.[5] He too traces toleration and its application through history, focusing especially on such figures as John Locke (about whom I say more below), to demonstrate that, historically, toleration was tied to societies that had a shared moral vision and a conscience, while today it is far more tightly tied to individual freedom. Instead of protecting minority groups as part of public policy for the common good, the enforced sanction of individual freedom encourages, ironically, the centralization of power and fosters indifference to values other than the value of tolerance itself.

Amy Chua's analysis of the history of tolerance is rather different. In her book *Day of Empire: How Hyperpowers Rise to Global Dominance — and Why They Fall,*[6] she argues that world empires — China's Tang Dynasty, Achaemenid Persia, Imperial Rome, the British Empire, the United States — demonstrate, in their expansion periods, a remarkable tolerance for pluralism and diversity, which has the effect of leveraging the contributions of all these diverse voices to enhance the empire itself. This is what she calls "strategic tolerance." The decline of an empire is marked by increasing desire to control everything and a consequent diminution of tolerance. The tipping point comes when enough people begin to rebel against the intolerance implicit in these restrictions, generating strife, discord, hatred, and violence — in short, the seeds of the decline and destruction of the empire.

This is the sort of sweeping thesis that has just enough plausibility to make a splash in the public square. There are enough historical holes in the work, however, to make one pause. In her treatment of the early period of any empire, Chua tends to lavish praise for every instance of tolerance while ignoring instances of intolerance — and then reverse the procedure for the later period. Doubtless the Romans were "progressive" in their day. In the time of Jesus, it was imperial policy to allow the diverse religions in the Empire to operate fairly

5. A. J. Conyers, *The Long Truce: How Toleration Made the World Safe for Power and Profit* (Waco: Baylor University Press, 2009).
6. New York: Anchor Books, 2007.

freely. Indeed, it was an offense, a capital offense, to desecrate a temple, any temple — the aim being, of course, to avoid major religious conflict. I suppose this is a kind of tolerance of diverse religions. Of course, the Romans also insisted on god-swaps: local conquered peoples were expected to accept some of the Roman gods into their own pantheon, while the Romans happily adopted some of the local gods into theirs. This god-swap might appear to be happily tolerant and ecumenical, but of course it was for the sake of stifling rebellion: if locals were tempted to throw off the Roman yoke, at the very least they could no longer count on the local gods to be only on their side. Moreover, once the Senate got into the habit of deifying deceased emperors and demanding that its citizens offer a pinch of incense to the deified Caesar, and, increasingly, to the deified *living* Caesar, the polytheists who made up most of the Empire had no difficulty complying. But was this strategic tolerance or Machiavellian manipulation? The Jews, of course, were an exception to Roman imperial policy, since they had no gods to swap and no figures representing gods. Worse, they stubbornly insisted that their God was Lord of all and that they were not going to offer incense to any Caesar, dead or alive. The Romans gritted their teeth and viewed them as miserably intransigent but not a big enough threat to squash, until, of course, A.D. 66-70 and again in the second century (A.D. 132-135). As long as Roman authorities perceived Christians to be a species of Jews, Christians could more or less hide under Jewish exceptionalism. When the divide between Jews and Christians became ever clearer, Christians faced repeated rounds of Roman persecution until about A.D. 300, when Constantine professed conversion to Christ. Indeed, it is often argued that emperors such as Trajan, who wanted to return the Empire to pagan discipline and who was therefore more brutal with Christians, and thus less tolerant, was nevertheless "better" for the Empire itself at that juncture, precisely because he imposed extra discipline — i.e., he was more *in*-tolerant. Life and Roman history are more subtle than Chua thinks.

As for her treatment of the United States, she praises the U.S. for being tolerant toward Jews and other Europeans, many of them scientists, who gained access to the country during Hitler's rise to power, and in consequence strengthened the U.S. and put it into a position where it could defeat the Axis powers. But she says nothing about

American internment of Japanese during World War II, at roughly the same period — scarcely an act of strategic tolerance. Indeed, at the time the internment was viewed as an act of wise strategic *in*tolerance. She lavishes praise on the U.S. for allowing and sometimes inviting so many people in the previous century to enter the country, citing this as early strategic tolerance, but tends to gloss over the treatment of Native Americans. Writing as she does toward the end of the Bush era, the focal point of her curiosity is how close America is to the loss of "strategic tolerance" and the adoption of intolerance that will spell its decline. But she exhibits no feel for the increasing polarization between the old tolerance and the new, and little grasp of how there is rising, ironically, an *increased* "tolerance" that is being (intolerantly) enforced by law on those who disagree! Similarly, unlike the works of Charles and Conyers, Chua's book neglects to place tolerance within a broader assumed moral vision framework.

Early Christian Thought

What is transparently obvious in all of these analyses is how every society mixes tolerance and intolerance in complex ways, a mix that is grounded in a certain moral vision, and all the pragmatic (and even corrupting) decisions that flow from that vision. This is true in the pagan world, the Christian world, and any other world for that matter. During the church's first three centuries or so, the dominant criticism Christians received from the diverse pagans of the Roman Empire was that their religion was too exclusive. Celsus, Porphyry, Symmachus, and many other scholarly pagans were happy to defend one branch of pagan thought against another, but none of them claimed to represent the *only* way to the divine. It follows that all of them took umbrage at the claim of Christians that Christ provides the *only* way to eternal life.

> All the ancient critics of Christianity were united in affirming that there is no one way to the divine. . . . It was not the kaleidoscope of religious practices and feelings that was the occasion for the discussion of religious pluralism in ancient Rome; it was the success

of Christianity, as well as its assertions about Christ and about Israel. . . . By appealing to a particular history as the source of knowledge of God, Christian thinkers transgressed the conventions that governed civilized theological discourse in antiquity.[7]

This antipathy toward Christians, all in the name of a more tolerant view of different (pagan) religions, inevitably constituted part of the backdrop that made the cycles of official Roman persecution of Christians — the most violent *in*tolerance — a morally acceptable pattern in the culture, until the numbers of Christians and the quality of their lives and sufferings began to modify public perception. Until that occurred, intolerance toward Christians was widely perceived as a virtue.

Not surprisingly, during the early centuries of the church's existence Christians could passionately defend tolerance. Toward the end of the second century, Tertullian of Carthage wrote, "It is a human law and a natural right that one should worship whatever he intends; the religious practice of one person neither harms nor helps another. It is no part of religion to coerce religious practice, for it is by free choice not coercion that we should be led to religion" (*To Scapula* 2.1-2). Again: "See that you do not give a reason for impious religious practice by taking away religious liberty and prohibit choice in divine matters, so that I may not worship as I wish, but am forced to worship what I do not wish" (*Apology* 24.6-10). About a century later, Lactantius wrote, "Religion is to be defended not by putting to death, but by dying, not by cruelty but by patience, not by an impious act but by faith. . . . For nothing is so much a matter of free will as religion [*Nihil est enim tam voluntarium quam religion*], for if the mind of the worshipper turns away it is carried off and nothing remains" (*Divine Institutes* 5.19). He goes on to say, "religion cannot be a matter of coercion [*religio cogi non potest*]"; it has to do with the will *(voluntas).*

With the Constantinian settlement, Christians suddenly found themselves allied with imperial power. Instead of being the disadvantaged religious community in the Empire, they now enjoyed the advantages of being associated with the emperor. That called forth new

---

7. Robert Louis Wilken, *Remembering the Christian Past* (Grand Rapids: Eerdmans, 1995), 42-43.

rounds of reflection on the relations between church and state and on the dynamic tension between tolerance and intolerance. Once Christianity became the official religion, believers were no longer in danger of officially sanctioned persecution; inevitably, however, they faced two new threats: (a) pressure from the state to be controlled by the state and (b) the temptation to pursue power for its own sake in a way that was impossible for them before the Christian profession of Constantine, or to use the power of the state to establish Christianity.

So far as we know, the first Christian leader to demand, by appealing to Scripture, the suppression of pagan cults was Firmicus Maternus in his *On the Error of Profane Religions* (c. A.D. 346). More influential by far was the authority of Augustine. His struggle against the Donatists, which occupied much of his energy in the late fourth and early fifth centuries, chronicles his shift in perspective. He became Bishop of Hippo in A.D. 395 and determined to end the ugly schism between Catholics and Donatists as expeditiously as possible. Initially he took only peaceful measures,[8] but in the early part of the fifth century his attitude changed. In part he was responding to violence against Catholics; in part he discovered that compulsory measures were often effective. Augustine remained implacably opposed to torture and physical coercion. Nevertheless, the stances he adopted toward the Donatists and the steps he took reshaped Christian understanding of how others should be treated. He deployed the command "compel them to come in" (Luke 14:23) from the parable of the great supper as sanction to enforce the submission of unbelievers and heretics (a formidable display of ripping a text out of its context); more importantly, he appealed to the civil authorities for help. "What death is worse for the soul than the liberty to err?" he asked *(To the Donatists)*. Augustine thus "established a precedent which fortified the practice of repression by the Medieval Church."[9] This is not to say that everyone followed Augustine's line. For instance, in A.D. 591 Gregory the Great wrote to Virgilius, Bishop of Arles, and to Theodore, Bishop of Marseilles, commending them for their zeal in evangelizing Jews, but criticizing them for the use of coercion instead of resorting

8. See, for instance, his *Tractates on John* 26.2.
9. H. Kamen, *The Rise of Toleration* (New York: McGraw-Hill, 1967), 14.

to "the sweetness of preaching." Nevertheless, Augustine's hardening position pointed the way for many church leaders in later centuries.

The Intolerant Road to Tolerance in the Modern Period

As the papacy increased in power across the centuries, and civil authorities waxed and waned, it sometimes became difficult to decide if the greatest threat came from Rome attempting to control kings and other rulers or from those rulers attempting to control Rome.[10] What is quite clear is that by the eleventh century "Europe *became* a persecuting society."[11] This did not happen overnight: for six centuries after Augustine, there is no record of execution on religious grounds. Nevertheless the great theologian's words provided some of the sanction for developments from the eleventh century on. The advice of some was relatively mild. Thomas Aquinas (1225-1274), for instance, in answer to the question as to whether unbelievers should be compelled to the faith, wrote,

> Among unbelievers there are some who have never received the faith, such as the heathens and the Jews; and these are by no means to be compelled to the faith, in order that they may believe, because to believe depends on the will: nevertheless they should be compelled by the faithful, if it be possible to do so, so that they do not hinder the faith by their blasphemies, or by their evil persuasions, or even by their persecutions.[12]

This, of course, is not exactly freedom of religion as it is currently understood in the West.

10. One of the most interesting recent books on the subject, that of Tom Holland (*The Forge of Christendom: The End of Days and the Epic Rise of the West* [New York: Doubleday, 2009]), argues, against much prevailing wisdom, that it was the influence of Gregory VII (c. A.D. 1015-1073) and his studied rebuffs of royal power that contributed most powerfully, in the long term, to later commitments to the separation of church and state.

11. R. I. Moore, *The Formation of a Persecuting Society: Power and Deviance in Western Europe, 950-1250* (Oxford: Oxford University Press, 1990), 5.

12. *Summa Theologica* I-II, 1.91, a.4.

The Middle Ages cough up many examples of more violent intolerance. The Papal Inquisition set up large numbers of tribunals throughout Europe. For example, in the late twelfth century Pope Lucius III sought to destroy the Albigensian heresy in southern France, an effort that continued for decades. One of these tribunals was set up in 1232 in the Kingdom of Aragon; there was never a tribunal set up by the Papal Inquisition in nearby Castile. In 1478, convinced that the Papal Inquisition was too weak, King Ferdinand II of Aragon and Queen Isabella I of Castile established the Spanish Inquisition — or, to give it its proper name, the Tribunal of the Holy Office of the Inquisition. It was designed to preserve Roman Catholic orthodoxy by replacing the tribunals under papal control. The Spanish Inquisition remained under the direct control of the Spanish monarchy until it was formally abolished in 1833.

In theory the Inquisition examined only Christians. Jews, Muslims, and other minorities did not come directly under its mandate. Such minorities often faced other highly discriminatory laws, but on occasion they could achieve positions of power in the nation. The Inquisition was most interested in examining *conversos* — mostly Jews, and later significant numbers of Muslims, who professed conversion to Catholicism but whose conversions were suspect. Jews were apparently converting in serious numbers, owing to fresh outbreaks of anti-Semitism; the Muslim Moors were converting, too, as their military forces had been thrown off the Spanish peninsula, leaving behind many Moors who were now ruled by the Spanish throne. The first six victims of the Inquisition were burned at the stake in 1481. The Inquisition was very active from about 1480 to 1530. Estimates vary, but probably no fewer than two thousand people met their death in similar fashion. Those who were found guilty by the tribunals were handed over to the secular authorities for punishment. Moreover, although the Inquisition focused on the *conversos* and had no direct authority over the unconverted Jews and Muslims of Spain, eventually it was decided that one of the things that tempted apparently converted Jews to live a dual life and maintain Jewish rites and customs was the presence of unconverted Jews — so attempts to banish all Jews from certain large Spanish cities followed.

None of this was done in the name of intolerance, of course. Undoubtedly some of the motives were ugly and corrupt: the lust for more power vested in the throne, the populism that finds it easy to blame minorities and stir up hate, even confiscating the goods of the wealthier victims. Part of the motivation was to preserve what the authorities felt was the true religion. What must be observed, however, is that this effort to preserve what was judged to be true religion was grounded not so much in argument in the marketplace of ideas as in coercion — coercion of the particularly powerful sort where church and state are so intertwined that the church uses the state to impose the most severe sanctions. In other words, it was not so much the commitment to a certain understanding of truth that brought about these excruciating results as the defense of the truth by the use of physical coercion backed up by the state.

One of the results of the Reformation was that Europe became divided between Catholic and Protestant states. By and large, Catholics did not tolerate Protestants, and Protestants did not tolerate Catholics: that is, on both sides there was a link between theological commitments and secular authority, for both sides were heirs to the medieval stance that presupposed that some degree of intolerance bathed in coercion was necessary to defend the truth. The culminating slaughter of the Thirty Years' War (1618-1648) brought incalculable horror. How much of this bloodshed was primarily a conflict generated by theologians arguing about truth, as opposed to rising nationalism, powerful fiefdoms, and lust for political independence, is much disputed. "The role religion had played in the war has always been a matter of some debate among historians. By 1648 it was more a matter of establishing rights to land; religion had been transmuted into moral geography."[13] But insofar as the wars were religious, they forced many people to conclude that there had to be a better way.[14] And as we shall see, the rising tolerance that was eventually spawned for groups belonging to minority religions did not come about through skepticism or apathy about religion, but sprang up, as much

---

13. Graham Ward, *True Religion* (Oxford: Blackwell, 2003), 60.

14. This is one of the themes of Diarmaid MacCulloch, *The Reformation: A History* (New York: Penguin, 2005).

THE INTOLERANCE OF TOLERANCE

as from anything else, through the refusal of minorities to be silenced and crushed.[15]

Notes on the Seventeenth and Eighteenth Centuries

The raging storms of intolerance, a substantial part of it religious, inevitably spawned renewed reflection on the justification and appropriate place of tolerance. The targets of the intolerance were many: Lollards, Albigensians, Anabaptists, Calvinists, Jews, Lutherans, Muslims, assorted Protestant separatists, and many others. Apart from wars between states, grounded in mutual distrust and intolerance, intolerance manifested itself *within* states by mandating, for dissidents, church attendance, banning their clergy, imprisonment, fines, required oaths of allegiance, restrictions on movements, social banning that made it difficult to find employment, various forms of public embarrassment, and, in the worst cases, torture and execution. One of the merits of Alexandra Walsham's study is that it demonstrates that at least until 1700 no religious group in the United Kingdom abandoned the ideal of religious uniformity.[16] In other words, rising appeals for toleration and gently escalating legislative acts of toleration were widely viewed as temporary measures to limit the violence until religious uniformity could be restored. Nevertheless this pattern was not reproduced everywhere. In the United Provinces (what came to be the Netherlands or Holland), there was much more breathing space for Mennonites and other Anabaptists, along with a variety of Unitarians and other heterodox thinkers, not to mention Jews from Spain.

The appeals for more toleration arose both from religious sec-

15. This is one of the important themes that repeatedly surfaces in Richard Bonney and D. J. B. Trim, eds., *Persecution and Pluralism: Calvinists and Religious Minorities in Early Modern Europe, 1550-1700* (Frankfurt am Main: Peter Lang, 2006).

16. Alexandra Walsham, *Charitable Hatred: Tolerance and Intolerance in England, 1500-1700* (Manchester: Manchester University Press, 2006). This stands over against the less nuanced and "straight line" reconstruction of scholars such as Perez Zagorin, *How the Idea of Religious Toleration Came to the West* (Princeton: Princeton University Press, 2003).

tors and from sectors that were perceived in the long haul to be more secularizing. In the former camp, some of the writings of John Owen stand out,[17] as does Roger Williams's *The Bloudy Tenet, of Persecution, for Cause of Conscience* (1644), which argues that no person should be prevented from worshiping according to his or her conscience. Unusual for a seventeenth-century Protestant, Williams was willing to grant such toleration to Jews, Muslims, Catholics, and any other religious group. More influential in the seventeenth century was John Milton's *Areopagetica* (published in November 1644, at the height of the English civil war), an impassioned defense of the principle of the right to freedom of speech and expression. Milton appeals to at least three controlling criteria: (1) the criterion of the public good, the view that any society will be a better society with augmented well-being if human autonomy is preserved and people can do and say and publish what they want to; (2) the criterion of promoting certain virtues — e.g., toleration fosters attentive listening to others, the virtue of self-criticism, and the like; (3) the criterion of epistemology — i.e., toleration is well suited to attaining well-grounded beliefs, to ascertaining the truth.

This certainly does not mean that all Christians were persuaded by Milton. Five years after the publication of Milton's *Areopagetica,* Samuel Rutherford (1600-1661), a Scottish Covenanting theologian and onetime Rector of St. Andrews University, published *A Free Disputation Against Pretended Liberty of Conscience* — essentially a response to Milton. All his life Rutherford sustained and nurtured a horror of pluralism, strengthened in him, perhaps, by his years in London where he spent time from 1643 to 1647 as one of the Scots Commissioners to the Westminster Assembly. Rutherford advocated that the civil magistrate — what we would call the power of the state — should be deployed to make people conform to true Christian doctrine, as adjudicated by the best judgment of the orthodox ministers of religion (which, of course, aligned with his own views). He insisted that such exertion of authority should be designed to compel *behav-*

---

17. See especially his "Indulgence and Toleration Considered" (1667), reprinted in his *Works* (London: Macmillan, 1850-53), 13.517-40, and other contributions in the same volume.

ioral conformity, for he insisted equally that heart and motive were known only to God. Moreover, he was self-critical enough to recognize that such a stance would likely foster hypocrisy, i.e., hypocritical religious behavior out of step with actual belief, even though he himself was one of the most pious and insistent advocates of true heart religion. The dissonance between his underscoring of the importance of heart religion and his insistence that the state should compel certain religious conformity was dissolved, in his view, in the importance of the public good: the magistrate's coercion might do no good to the one compelled to conform, but it would diminish the number of bad examples and unsound teachers in the community and thus protect the community.

Paul Helm helpfully argues that Rutherford was not entirely wrong.[18] Rutherford was correct to perceive that the toleration at issue was not over matters of convenience (such as putting up with, i.e., tolerating, a noisy neighbor) but had an epistemological dimension — that is, the issues at stake were truth claims; they were matters that could be disputed as to their reasonableness and truth. Rutherford judged that intolerance was in this case good because the beliefs of his opponents were both erroneous and dangerous. Helm argues that, while Rutherford was wrong to advocate intolerance, he was right to perceive the nature of the issue: matters of religion do not turn on mere subjective feelings, but on issues of truth and falsity. The issues are neither trivial nor socially inconsequential. The problem is that Rutherford argues from the infallibility of Scripture, and, implicitly, the (self-perceived) infallibility of his understanding of Scripture, to intolerance. One cannot legitimately defend intolerance by an appeal to infallibility, however, when that very claim to infallibility is precisely what is being challenged. And if one persists in this tactic, one is forced to concede that one's opponents are justified in *their* intolerance, when *they* are in power, granted that *they* perceive the infallibility of their own position, grounded in different authority.

The point to observe in these debates between, on the one hand,

18. Paul Helm, "Rutherford and the Limits of Toleration," in *Tolerance and Truth: The Spirit of the Age or the Spirit of God?* ed. Angus Morrison, Edinburgh Dogmatics Conference Papers (Edinburgh: Rutherford House, 2007), 57-74.

Williams, Owen, and Milton, and, on the other, Rutherford, is that tolerance and intolerance were being debated in the framework of larger issues about the common good, about the nature of truth and authority, about the relationship between church and state. That is one of the reasons why political steps in many countries were piecemeal, as authorities were trying to get the balance of things right. By contemporary standards, the 1689 Act of Toleration in England left much to be desired, but it was groundbreaking at the time. It granted the right of worship to Nonconformists provided they pledged allegiance to the Crown and rejected transubstantiation (Catholics and, for that matter, non-Trinitarians were excluded from the Act). They could meet in their own approved places of worship, but they were excluded from public office and from the universities. Forty years earlier, the Act of Toleration passed by the Maryland colony granted freedom of religion for all Trinitarian believers, but promised capital punishment for those who denied the deity of Jesus. A decade earlier, what became the state of Rhode Island passed more sweeping laws that promised tolerance even for non-Trinitarians and established the first political model of what is now called the separation of church and state. All of this may seem terribly slow and inconsistent from our vantage point, but when one contrasts the events of the French Revolution, a century after the English Act of Toleration, and its sweeping away of all religious restraint, climaxing in the triumph of Madame Guillotine, one may conscientiously plump for change by degrees.[19]

In the long term, another group of thinkers, trending toward what would become more secularizing thought, exerted greater influence on later developments than the Christian thinkers just described. John Locke (1632-1704) published his *Letter Concerning Toleration* in 1689. Thirty years earlier, in his *Essay in Defence of the Good Old Cause,* Locke had argued that religious toleration was impractical and dangerous because it would foster civil unrest. At the time he wrote his *Letter,* however, England was still being tossed hither and yon by the impact of the Glorious Revolution and the Restoration, not

---

19. For a comparison of the American and French Revolutions and their respective "takes" on religion, cf. Carson, *Christ and Culture Revisited* (Grand Rapids: Eerdmans, 2008), esp. 186-90.

to mention conflict between the Church of England and the Dissenters and ongoing fears that a Catholic heir might come to the throne. Now Locke argued that both history and human nature show that toleration is actually necessary for civil order:

> It is not the diversity of Opinions, (which cannot be avoided) but the refusal of toleration to those that are of different Opinions, (which might have been granted) that has produced all the Bustles and Wars, that have been in the Christian World, upon account of Religion. The heads and Leaders of the Church, moved by Avarice and insatiable desire of Dominion, making use of the immoderate Ambition of Magistrates, and the credulous Superstition of the giddy Multitude, have incensed and animated them against those that dissent from themselves: by preaching unto them, contrary to the Laws of the Gospel and to the Precepts of Charity, That Schismaticks and Hereticks are to be outed of their Possessions, and destroyed.[20]

Of course, Locke, along with other thinkers of his time, was developing the metaphysical dualism of René Descartes. The realm of the subject (mind or soul) is private, invisible, and inaccessible; the realm of the object is "out there" and is observable in line with rational objective principles. In Locke's adaptation, we must recognize that each individual is a unique union of these realms, forcing us to accept the dualism of the external and political realm of power and the internal religious realm of faith in which no coercion has any legitimate place. This dualism, this fundamental contrast between the objective public sphere and the subjective private sphere, has become one of the foundations of many contemporary notions of religious toleration and religious liberty.

We shall have reason, a little later on in this book, to query the public/private dualism. At the moment we cannot help but remember that, rather notoriously, Locke argued for intolerance toward Catholics and atheists for reasons of public order: Catholics could not be trusted since they owe allegiance to a foreign prince (the pope), and

---

20. John Locke, *Letter Concerning Toleration*, ed. J. H. Tully (Indianapolis: Hackett, 1983 [orig. 1689]), 55.

atheists could not be trusted because those who do not believe in divine rewards and punishments have insufficient motives for faithfulness. In principle, however, Locke was advocating the separation of church and state, even if his own application was spotty and his undergirding metaphysics is suspect.

Before we reflect on what this potted history contributes to our assessment of contemporary tolerance, we must enter a few observations on more recent developments.

More Recent Developments

John Stuart Mill (1806-1873), British philosopher and civil servant, accepted something of the same dualism as did Locke but was a proponent of Utilitarianism. In his famous *On Liberty* (1859), Mill asserts that intolerance is so natural to human beings that religious freedom owes more to growing religious indifference than to principle.[21] If, however, a principle is to be established, one "very simple principle" will suffice, namely, "the sole end for which mankind are warranted, individually or collectively, in interfering with the liberty of action of any of their number is self-protection."[22] The idea is that adopting such a stance and abjuring the use of coercion when one has the power to coerce is the best safeguard against being coerced when one does not have the power. This is highly utilitarian, of course, and more than a little naive. After all, even the agents of the Inquisition thought that they were protecting society. That is why Mill also deploys his controversial distinction between conduct that concerns others and conduct that concerns only oneself — his update on the distinction between the public, objective sphere and the private, subjective sphere.[23] Inevitably he relegates more religious and many moral matters (even monogamy!) to the latter.[24] Combine these stances with the growing nineteenth-century respect for the rights and autonomy of

21. J. S. Mill, *On Liberty* (Indianapolis: Hackett, 1978 [orig. 1859]), 8.
22. Mill, *On Liberty,* 9.
23. Mill, *On Liberty,* 73.
24. Mill, *On Liberty,* 89.

the individual conscience, and one begins to understand the nature of contemporary commitments to tolerance.

Mill introduced a further innovation: he offered a positive appreciation of diversity. As Edward Langerak observes, "Locke was not the one to celebrate diversity: he merely argued the irrationality of not enduring it. . . . Beginning with Mill, however, we see arguments not simply for enduring diversity as conducive to peace or progress, but also for celebrating, approving, and affirming it. Thus he claimed that public opinion, and not just legal coercion, was an undesirable constraint on human flourishing."[25] "Indeed, he argued that society's being judgmental about diversity maimed individuals in a way similar to the Chinese practice of foot-binding."[26] This has led to the increasing perception that

> tolerance sometimes connotes broad-minded approval of important differences and not merely the tendency to put up with them. . . . Mill and some liberals may underestimate how personal integrity and group identity require the judgment that many important differences are disagreeably wrong, even if tolerable. One may be able to welcome any number of ethnic, cultural, and lifestyle diversities as adding spice to a pleasing pluralism and yet regard many moral and religious differences as sad and disagreeable wrongs that one should argue against even while tolerating them.[27]

Four observations on developments in the wake of Mill bring us not only to the present day but also to the conclusion of this chapter.

First, what began as complicated and sometimes nuanced debates about (1) the ways in which tolerance and intolerance should be worked out so as to promote the public good, (2) how to affirm truth and protect people from untruth (especially when various sides have differing visions of what the truth is), and (3) the extent to which the church should or should not appeal to the civil magistrates to enforce

---

25. Edward Langerak, "Theism and Toleration," in Quinn and Taliaferro, eds., *A Companion to Philosophy of Religion,* 518-19; referring to Mill, *On Liberty,* 9.

26. Langerak, "Theism and Toleration," 519; referring to Mill, *On Liberty,* 66.

27. Langerak, "Theism and Toleration," 519.

ecclesiastical stances increasingly became a discussion about the appropriate relationship between church and state.

The important thing to recognize is that Christianity itself has rich theological resources to think through these things in biblical categories. These resources include Jesus' famous words, "Give back to Caesar what is Caesar's and to God what is God's" (Mark 12:17; cf. John 18:36), and the principled running tension between Christian requirements to submit to the state because it is ordained by God (Romans 13:1-7) and the Christian recognition that sometimes the state is a persecuting beast (e.g., Revelation 13; 19), between the biblical obligation to seek the peace and prosperity of the city (Jeremiah 29:7) and the biblical expectation that believers will face persecution (John 15:18–16:4; Revelation 13:7). Moreover, Christians have regularly demanded fair treatment of human beings on the ground that human beings have been created in the image of God. Further, at their best Christians have insisted that truth borne along by the Holy Spirit has the power to illumine and convert, while state-imposed sanctions achieve, at best, external conformity but no regeneration. I have dealt with such matters at some length elsewhere[28] and therefore need not repeat that material here. The issues are complicated, but perhaps three further reflections on the separation of church and state should be entered before we leave this first observation.

(1) Owing not least to the kinds of utterances just quoted from the Bible, Christianity has *always,* at some level, wrestled with the relationship between church and state. For the first three centuries of the church's life, of course, Christians were a minority in the Roman Empire, often a persecuted minority. But even with the conversion of Constantine, bishops continued on occasion to rebuke emperors (as Ambrose rebuked Theodosius in the fourth century). The complex interplay between popes and monarchs during the Middle Ages reminds us that power was never vested in only one domain. All sides acknowledge that there has been much more self-conscious Christian reflection on the relationships between church and state since the seventeenth century than there was in earlier centuries. Nevertheless, the history of the church, not only in Europe but elsewhere, reminds

---

28. Carson, *Christ and Culture Revisited,* esp. chap. 5.

us that the distinction between church and state is intrinsic to the Scriptures that govern Christians. At the most basic level, we recall that the locus of God's people in the Old Testament, under the old covenant, was a nation, the nation of Israel, while the locus of God's people in the New Testament, under the new covenant, is *not* a nation, but the church — an international community of believers never entirely identified with any nation.

(2) That does not mean that the equilibrium between church and state has always been clear, or even agreed. Many Americans think the terminology is embedded in the U.S. Constitution, but of course that is not so. The First Amendment states, "Congress shall make no law respecting an establishment of religion or prohibiting the free exercise thereof; or abridging the freedom of speech, or of the press; or the right of the people peaceably to assemble, and to petition the government for a redress of grievances." Arguably "the establishment of religion" about which Congress shall make no law had in view, at the time, the fact that some states already had an "established" religion: Connecticut, for instance, was tied to the Congregational Church, and Congress was not to meddle in such matters. The expression "building a wall of separation between Church & State" first appears in a letter Thomas Jefferson wrote to the Baptist Association of Danbury in 1802. It entered the vocabulary of Supreme Court decisions in 1878 *(Reynolds v. United States),* though it exercised little clout until the landmark case of *Everson v. Board of Education* in 1947.[29]

Yet it is important to see that many Western nations that still have an established church (e.g., England, Denmark) enjoy as much freedom of religion as Americans do (though it is shaped a little differently) and think of themselves as tolerant cultures. Meanwhile France, whose revolution in 1789, as some wag has put it, did not so much secure freedom *of* religion as freedom *from* religion, promotes many barriers between church and state.[30]

One of the effects, for good and ill, of the varied developments

29. I outlined these and other developments in greater detail in *Christ and Culture Revisited,* 173-84.

30. See *Christ and Culture Revisited,* 185-90. Cf. Thomas Albert Howard, "The Dialectic and the Double Helix," *First Things* 211 (March 2011): 21-25.

regarding the relationships between church and state is the almost inevitable and certainly incessant pressure to restrict religion to private domains. We start by insisting that the state can neither establish nor prohibit religion, and agree that, reciprocally, religion does not have the right to control the state. Then in a mighty bound many infer further that religion does not have the right to influence any of the decisions of the state, and therefore conclude that religion must be restricted to a small and privatized world or the great barrier between church and state is jeopardized.[31] If this conclusion were ruthlessly carried out, millions of citizens would be disenfranchised on hundreds of topics, as we shall see. What seems like a simple and useful ideal — the separation of church and state — is suddenly fraught with widely accepted cultural assumptions that few thinking Christians could ever accept.

(3) Discussion about the relationships between church and state becomes staggeringly more difficult when we abandon Christian assumptions and enter the world of Islam. Many have noted that Islam has no theological resources on which to draw so as to think freshly about the relationships between church and state. There is no utterance, for instance, akin to "Give back to Caesar what is Caesar's and to God what is God's" (Mark 12:17).[32] This does not mean that Islam has exhibited no strains of tolerance. Historically, some caliphates have been more tolerant than others. In the last century-and-a-half or so, a minority of Muslim scholars have argued that the important *jihad* is not the fight against external enemies but the spiritual struggle within. As some Muslims move to Western countries where questions of tolerance occupy more space in public discussion, it is not surprising to read important essays like that of Ismail Acar, "Theological Foundations of Religious Tolerance in Islam: A Qur'anic Perspective."[33] What is fascinating about such exercises, as welcome as they

31. Cf. D. A. Carson, *The Gagging of God: Christianity Confronts Pluralism* (Grand Rapids: Zondervan, 1996), 347-48, 404.

32. Carson, *Christ and Culture Revisited,* 191-203.

33. In *Religious Tolerance in World Religions,* ed. Jacob Neusner and Bruce Chilton (West Conshohocken: Templeton Foundation Press, 2008), 297-313. Cf. also M. A. Muqtedar Khan, "American Muslims and the Rediscovery of America's Sacred Ground," in *Taking Religious Pluralism Seriously: Spiritual Politics on America's Sacred*

are, is that they *never,* as far as I can see, explore the relationships between church and state. They envisage how devout Muslims might properly live in the West; they conjure up how Muslim states have treated, or might or ought to treat, religious minorities in the name of Allah the Merciful. But they do not envisage a church and a state operating in somewhat different domains. "Islamic fundamentalism, uninfluenced by the Western debate about the separation of church and state, a question it may find unintelligible . . . , contends that the religious law *(Shari a)* of the Qur'an does not distinguish theological from moral or political grounds for law and thus is normative for a country's legislation."[34] Indeed, the entire notion is likely to seem vaguely blasphemous to them: the understanding of the nation-state that developed in eighteenth-century Europe is largely alien to much Muslim thought, while the notion of a "church" or of different denominational "churches" is entirely foreign. The people *(ummah)* of Allah are not easily differentiable from the people who constitute Muslim nations; the law of Islam applies to every domain of life (including the state), and Allah brooks no rivals. How then shall one drive a wedge between church and state? Moreover, privatized religion is incomprehensible and incoherent to most Muslims who have never lived in the West, and not infrequently unattractive to those who do. In a well-written and influential work, Shabbir Akhtar, who lectures at Old Dominion University in Virginia, argues that ultimately Islam will (and ought to) win worldwide domination, because Islam alone, and certainly not Christianity, is internally constituted to be an imperial religion.[35]

The importance of this observation becomes clearer when we recognize that expressions such as "freedom of religion" mean very different things in different parts of the world. In the West and in some other parts of the world, it presupposes not only the freedom to practice one's religion without let or hindrance, but equal status before the law, freedom to convert to another religion or no religion, and

---

Ground, ed. Barbara A. McGraw and Jo Renee Formicola (Waco: Baylor University Press, 2005), 127-47.

34. Langerak, "Theism and Toleration," 520.

35. Shabbir Akhtar, *Islam as Political Religion: The Future of an Imperial Faith* (London: Routledge, 2011).

freedom to proselytize in favor of one's religion within the bounds of open debate and dissemination of information and arguments.[36] But in most Muslim nations, and certainly wherever *Shari a* law is applied, non-Muslims may convert to Islam, but Muslims may not convert to anything else. There will always be sanctions, and in the most extreme cases the sanction is death. The claim that Islam at its heart is already a religion of peace and tolerance does not stand up very well if one applies this simple twofold test: (a) Are members of the *ummah*, the people of Islam, free to convert to some other religion without fear of sanctions? (b) May members of *any* religion or no religion propagate their beliefs as openly as Muslims do?[37]

Once one understands these realities, the perennial accounts of what happens to Muslims who wish to abandon Islam are understandable. After becoming a "democracy," in the sense that its citizens had cast a democratic vote,[38] Afghanistan, whose constitution is based on *Shari a* law, prosecuted Abdul Rahman for the crime of abandoning Islam when he became a Christian in 2006. The death penalty would have been imposed had it not been for massive international pressure. Rahman was released in March 2006 and accepted asylum in Italy. In Muslim countries where the interpretation of *Shari a* law is not so strict (e.g., Malaysia), the sanction imposed on,

36. Cf. Article 18 of the United Nations' Declaration of Human Rights: "Everyone has the right to freedom of thought, conscience and religion; this right includes freedom to change his religion or belief, and freedom, either alone or in community with others and in public or private, to manifest his religion or belief in teaching, practice, worship and observance."

37. The failure to address such questions adequately is what weakens the argument of Stephen Schwartz, *The Two Faces of Islam: The House of Sa ud from Tradition to Terror* (New York: Doubleday, 2002). He lays virtually all the blame for Islamic terror on what he calls "the fascistic Wahhabi cult" as a late-developing perversion of Islam. What percentage of the incentives to attempt international influence by means of terror can be laid at the door of Wahhabism is a complex issue, and Schwartz may well be more right than wrong. Yet it does not follow that Islam *apart from Wahhabism* is religiously tolerant if one applies the twin tests articulated above.

38. This is, of course, an example of the fact that democracy, in the richest sense, demands more than occasional or regular democratic elections, but also such structures as equal protection under the law, an independent judiciary, freedom of the press, and limited government (itself subject to constitutional constraints, whether the constitution be written or oral).

say, Malays who abandon Islam in favor of another religion will certainly include lengthy spells of enforced indoctrination, possibly prison terms, and a variety of social and fiscal restrictions. For example, two ex-Muslims converted to Christianity will not be able to marry, because they remain registered as Muslims and may marry only as Muslims (even though Chinese Malaysians who are registered from birth as Buddhists or Christians may marry their co-religionists). In Jordan, the North Amman Shari'a Court annulled the marriage of Mohammad Abbad, a Muslim convert to Christianity, on the ground that "marriage depends on the [Muslim] creed, and the apostate has no creed" (22 May 2008). This result stands even though Jordan's constitution affirms freedom of religion, and its penal code does not specifically outlaw apostasy. More broadly, when world leaders fear violence, bombings, and widespread killings because of the prospect of burning a copy of the Qur'an, but do not fear that there will be violence, bombings, and widespread killings because of the prospect of burning a copy of the Bible, what does that tell you about the tolerance levels of the two respective religions?

To summarize: the first observation on developments since John Stuart Mill is that much of the controversy about the nature of tolerance and intolerance has come to revolve around what is meant by the separation of church and state, a notion that has regularly been defended by Christians from their study of the Bible. Yet the notion of the separation of church and state, as valuable as it is, has come to mean quite different things in different sectors of the West, including, very often, the privatization of religion, while in some parts of the world the concept is incoherent.

Second, the processes of secularization have, as it were, flipped a cultural switch. This claim needs unpacking.

Secularization is a highly debated topic.[39] Neither the forces behind secularization nor its meaning are widely agreed upon. The recent magisterial volume by Charles Taylor canvases the options superbly.[40] Most hold that nineteenth-century Europe throws up the

39. Most recently, see the useful essay by Slavica Jakelic, "Secularism: A Bibliographical Essay," *Hedgehog Review* 12, no. 3 (2010): 49-55.

40. Charles Taylor, *A Secular Age* (Cambridge: Belknap, 2007). Much more briefly, see his "The Meaning of Secularism," *Hedgehog Review* 12, no. 3 (2010): 23-34.

most pivotal forces that drive the movement.[41] The political ethic at the heart of secularism

> can be and is shared by people of very different basic outlooks (what Rawls calls "comprehensive views of the good"). A Kantian will justify the rights to life and freedom by pointing to the dignity of rational agency; a Utilitarian will speak of the necessity to treat beings who can experience joy and suffering in such a way as to maximize the first and minimize the second; and a Christian will speak of humans as made in the image of God. They concur on the principles, but differ on the deeper reasons for holding to this ethic. The state must uphold the ethic, but must refrain from favoring any of the deeper reasons.[42]

Most scholars today also concur that these forces do not necessarily mean the abolition of religion; rather, secularization may squeeze religion away from the public sectors of politics, the media, and the academic world, into the purely private sectors. By some assessments, a nation may become more secularized and more religious at the same time. It's just that the religious side does not matter very much anymore in the public square and therefore in the direction of the nation, in its public pulse.

The switch that these cultural developments have flipped lies in the domain of presuppositions. Until the early part of the nineteenth century, the overwhelming majority of people in Europe and of European descent presupposed the existence of God. That meant that questions about tolerance and intolerance had to be worked out within the framework of this presupposition, within the framework of what people thought about God. By the end of the century, however, a cultural switch was flipped: either people did not presuppose the existence of God, or, if they did, they no longer presupposed that he was immediately relevant to all the questions raised in the public square. That in turn meant that questions about tolerance and intolerance had to be worked out within grids that were either non-theistic or

---

41. Cf. Owen Chadwick, *The Secularization of the European Mind in the Nineteenth Century* (Cambridge: Cambridge University Press, 1975).
42. Taylor, "The Meaning of Secularism," 25.

whose theism was so attenuated by the rising forces of secularization that they exercised little control.

That recognition leads us to the next observation.

Third, the twentieth century, the bloodiest in human history, exhibited spectacular instances of intolerance — and the most violent exemplars had very little to do with religion. Of course, there was at least a religious component in the strife in the Balkans and again in the bloody violence between Tutsis and Hutus. Yet most observers recognized that even here the more important factors were tribalism, racism, perceived economic injustice, very different interpretations of history, and "honor" and vengeance killings that escalated to the scale of genocide.

Few religious factors played much part in the largest of the slaughters of the twentieth century, the violence espoused by Fascism and Communism.[43] Perhaps fifty million Chinese died under Mao, about twenty million Ukrainians under Stalin, and then we come to World War II and the Holocaust. In both its Russian and its Chinese forms, Communism was overtly atheistic. In both its German and its Italian forms, Fascism was nominally Christian but only in the sense that it was happy to appeal to God and religion in pursuit of its own social and political agendas, never so as to be reformed by Scripture or Christian truth or morality, never in any sense to belong to the great tradition of historic creeds. Despite the best efforts of Jonathan I. Israel not only to ground the Enlightenment in the thought of Spinoza but also to demonstrate that *only* atheism provides adequate resources to generate toleration — in his analysis, theism and religious belief in all their forms are intrinsically intolerant[44] — the outcome in

43. See especially Meic Pearse, *The Gods of War: Is Religion the Primary Cause of Violent Conflict?* (Downers Grove: InterVarsity, 2007).

44. See especially Jonathan I. Israel, *Radical Enlightenment: Philosophy and the Making of Modernity, 1650-1750* (New York: Oxford University Press, 2002); idem, *Enlightenment Contested: Philosophy, Modernity, and the Emancipation of Man, 1670-1752* (New York: Oxford University Press, 2009); idem, *A Revolution of Mind: Radical Enlightenment and the Intellectual Origins of Modern Democracy* (Princeton: Princeton University Press, 2009). Jonathan Israel's commitment to the thesis that *only* atheism generates tolerance drives him to conclude that Pierre Bayle (1647-1706), whose essay on Luke 14:23 ("Compel them to come in") helped to overturn the Augustinian consensus that wrongly uses this verse to justify coercion, had to be a skeptic or an atheist. The

the twentieth century is scarcely reassuring. Atheism, whether theoretical (as in Communism) or practical (as in Fascism), far from being tolerant, spilled oceans of blood.

It is not hard to see why. In both cases, the defenders and rulers of these systems firmly believed that they were defending the truth of a large system of thought that supported the greater good. Whether, on the one hand, Marxist dialectic, an essentially economic analysis of human dilemmas, and the urgent need for Revolutionary Man to prepare the way for the New Man, or, on the other, the demand for discipline, the ideal of the one pure *Volk,* and confidence that most evils were tied to despicable Jews and other abominable elements, there was no authority capable of questioning the authority of the state. Even in the bloodiest of the religious wars in Europe, there were competing authority centers. By contrast, under both Communism and Fascism the authority of the state was totalitarian.

From the perspective of the larger thesis of this chapter, we observe, once again, that tolerance and intolerance were worked out *within the framework of a larger system of thought.* Granted, say, the truth of Marxism-Leninism, how much lenience could the state legitimately extend? In other words, neither tolerance nor intolerance was viewed as an independent virtue or vice, but as an arrangement to be worked out within the framework of the dominant system of thought.

Fourth, regardless of the widespread inability to agree on what it is, postmodernism has exerted incalculable influence in much of the world. Disagreement over the essence of postmodernism cannot blind us to its effect. Almost all sides agree that *as a movement* postmodernism is dead. Except in some American undergraduate programs, its luminaries are no longer read — certainly not in Europe, whence most of them sprang. Yet the effluents of postmodernism, however defined, are still very much with us, shaping our thoughts and cultural values. What cannot be denied is that, in its wake, countless millions of people find it difficult, at least on some subjects, to think in terms of truth and error, much preferring to

careful work of John D. Woodbridge, "Pierre Bayle: Protestant Contributor to Religious Toleration?" (forthcoming in *First Things*), demonstrates the overwhelming likelihood that Bayle remained a Protestant in the Reformed tradition when he wrote his essay on Luke 14:23.

think in terms of differences of opinion, of varying perspectives. The dawning of postmodernism coincided, at least in part, with the increasing diversification of the populations of many of the world's metropolises. The impact of this increasing empirical pluralism is multiplied many times over by the digital revolution: with minimal effort we find ourselves exposed to an incredibly broad diversity of cultures, opinions, interpretations of history, languages, and so forth. Moreover, in the virtual world we can create our own realities. All of this conspires to push questions of truth to the margins while magnifying the importance of tolerance.

It is not as if everyone has shifted from the paradigm of modernism to the effluents of postmodernism. Within our universities, for example, there is considerable diversity. Thinkers operating with a postmodern epistemology are more likely to be found in English, sociology, anthropology, and religion departments, and often history departments, than in physics, chemistry, engineering, and computer science departments. Lecturers in the latter departments are often unreconstructed modernists — or, still more commonly, they are modernists with respect to their own disciplines, but postmodernists in the arenas of ideology, religion, and morality. Transparently, postmodernism has softened somewhat in the last ten years or so (twenty-five years in continental Europe), as the weaknesses and absurdities of its more extreme forms have become transparent to many. Regardless of the terminology, pragmatism now commonly eclipses both nature and religion as cultural authority.[45] But if in its most aggressive forms postmodernism has declined, it has left a residue of subjective eclecticism that fosters the elevation of tolerance to the enthroned status of supreme virtue.

This is not to say that postmodernism has single-handedly *caused* this elevation of tolerance. If the survey provided in this chapter has any validity, it demonstrates how complex and intertwined are the historical and cultural movements that bring about tectonic shifts in cultural perception. Not least in America, the relevant forces were in play long before the rise of popular postmodernism. When Dietrich

45. This is one of the central theses of Roger Lundin, *From Nature to Experience: The American Search for Cultural Authority* (New York: Rowman & Littlefield, 2007).

Bonhoeffer visited America in the 1930s and tried to make sense of the American church scene, "he was fascinated that tolerance trumped truth."[46] Coming as he did from continental Europe, it is easy to understand why Bonhoeffer read the American scene that way. Whether or not that reading was entirely right at the time, there can be little doubt that the impact of postmodernism since the 1930s, plus the globalization of much of the world and certainly of many of the world's metropolises (with both good and bad effects), have reinforced the perception that tolerance has trumped truth, at least in this sense: for the first time in history, tolerance is today rarely perceived to be something that has to be worked out for the good of society *within* the matrix of a widely adopted system of truth and morals; it is now perceived as an independent virtue, perhaps the highest virtue.

Concluding Reflections

One of the clearest thinkers on this subject is J. Daryl Charles:

> Tolerance in its conception took on the cast of a virtue because of its concern for the common good and its respect for people as persons. We endure particular customs, behaviors or habits — sometimes even (relatively) bad habits — of people in the interest of preserving a greater unity. In the Lockean context, tolerance was advocated for religious non-conformists. Never was it construed, however, to imply — much less to sanction — morally questionable behavior. Consider, however, the devolution of a concept. What was a public virtue in its prior state becomes a vice if and when it ceases to care for truth, ignores the common good, and disdains the values that uphold a community. The culture of "tolerance" in which we presently find ourselves is a culture in which people believe nothing, possess no clear concept of right and wrong, and are remarkably indifferent to this precarious state of affairs. As a result of this transmutation, "tolerance" becomes indistinguishable from an intractably intolerant relativism. The

46. Eric Metaxas, *Bonhoeffer: Pastor, Martyr, Prophet, Spy* (Nashville: Nelson, 2010), 338.

challenge facing people of faith is learning how to purify tolerance so that it remains a virtue without succumbing to the centripetal forces of relativism and the spirit of the age.[47]

The new tolerance, then, has become a supreme virtue, if not *the* supreme virtue, of much of the Western world and beyond. No longer a function of a broader ethical and moral cultural consensus, tolerance is not worked out in terms of what might be *permitted* — legally, intellectually, socially — granted the "givens" of this broader consensus, but becomes an absolute good that gains the power to erode other cultural distinctives, including moral and religious distinctives. In the mind of many observers, this new tolerance thereby rushes in to support moral relativism. Because of its independent status, this new tolerance becomes, ironically, a *moralizing* support of moral relativism. One of the purposes of this chapter has been to show how great a change this is from the understanding and function of tolerance in the past, when tolerance was not perceived to be an intellectual stance but a social response.

In addition to the ways these changes in our understanding of tolerance have affected Western culture, we need to become aware of how people in other cultures are reading these changes. In his book *Why the Rest Hates the West: Understanding the Roots of Global Rage,*[48] Meic Pearse spells out how this new understanding of tolerance is perceived to be a threat to other cultures:

> The currency of the term *tolerance* has recently become badly debased. Where it used to mean the respecting of real, hard differences, it has come to mean instead a dogmatic abdication of truth-claims and a moralistic adherence to moral relativism — departure from either of which is stigmatized as intolerance. . . . Where the old tolerance allowed hard differences on religion and morality to rub shoulders and compete freely in the public square, the new variety wishes to lock them all indoors as matters of private judgment; the public square must be given over to indistinct-

---

47. J. Daryl Charles, "Truth, Tolerance, and Christian Conviction: Reflections on a Perennial Question — a Review Essay," *Christian Scholar's Review* 36 (2007): 212.
48. Downers Grove: InterVarsity, 2004.

ness. If the old tolerance was, at least, a real value, the new, intolerant "tolerance" might better be described as an antivalue; it is a disposition of hostility to any suggestion that one thing is "better" than another, or even that any way of life needs protected space from its alternatives.[49]

The result is that this new tolerance tends to stifle and subdue the distinctive claims of other cultures. The antivalue of this new tolerance dilutes and destroys all the hard and otherwise unyielding components of cultural identity, for they are judged to be marks of intolerance. The West, not least with its fiscal and digital power, is perceived by many to be culture-destroying, superficial, self-righteous, parading superiority because of its "tolerance," while that very tolerance destroys everything that disagrees with it. The charge may not be entirely fair, but it is very widespread.

If the potted history in this chapter brings the innovative and dangerous nature of this new tolerance into clearer focus, the next chapter shows that this new tolerance regularly indulges in the kind of inconsistency that makes it even more dangerous than it might otherwise be.

---

49. Pearse, *Why the Rest Hates the West*, 12.

FOUR

Worse Than Inconsistency

—◦◦◦—

The confusion of the two rather different meanings of "tolerance" — the older meaning according to which one disagreed with another's stance but, within the matrix of a broader ethical vision, insisted the other had the right to express his or her views; and the newer meaning according to which one should not disagree with or disparage another's views, very often with this "tolerance" being assumed to be the highest good — leads to many confusing discussions. We flip back and forth between the two uses of tolerance and fail to perceive that we have done so. What is worse, these two meanings of tolerance are not absolutely disjunctive: there is a nasty area of overlap that magnificently muddies the discussion.

Consider, for example, the charge raised by many on the left to the effect that the right is fundamentally intolerant, especially the religious right. On this view, people on the right are characterized (caricatured?) as "the pit bulls of the culture wars — small brains, big teeth, strong jaws, and no interest in compromise" (as Daniel Taylor nicely puts it).[1] It would be pleasant to dismiss these charges as nothing more than the intemperate and hypocritically intolerant rantings of the left; it would be even more pleasant if we could seriously affirm that such rantings invariably reflect the second meaning of intolerance.

1. "Deconstructing the Gospel of Tolerance," *Christianity Today* 43, no. 1 (11 January 1999): 48.

But then reality sets in. *First,* on some issues the right *does* want legal sanctions against practices it judges to be hugely damaging to society at large. For example, most on the right (and not a few on the left, for that matter) think that the law should prohibit third-trimester abortions, with penalties for those who defy the law. Similarly, while they may think that whatever consenting homosexual adults do in their bedrooms should be beyond the sanction of law, many also think that to grant the status of "marriage" to homosexual unions is foolish, short-sighted, and damaging to society. Perhaps, they might argue, the oft-proposed "marriage amendment" is the only answer. When the left labels the right as "intolerant" on such matters, it may be because they view the tolerance/intolerance issue as the absolute good. To that extent, the right *ought* to challenge them. Yet strictly speaking, on these issues the right is intolerant *in the first sense* — based on the older meaning of tolerance: that is, it views the issues in question as moral matters that deserve the discrimination of the state, including an appropriate penal code. What the right ought to say on such matters is something like this: "Of course we are intolerant on these matters — just as we are intolerant of pedophilia, rape, and other evils where in our view we are dealing with moral matters that deserve the discrimination of the state."

But *second,* sometimes the right sounds off about issues that few if any would want to be sorted out by rewriting the penal code — for example, the ideal of limited government or certain economic policies. The rhetoric may be so heated on the right that those who disagree may be branded as nitwits, idiots, or even traitors to American ideals, if not to the Constitution. The left may then respond by saying that the right is intolerant. (I hasten to add that this example could easily reverse "left" and "right" by choosing a different example without loss to its relevance!) Once again, by the charge of intolerance the left may be thinking of intolerance in the second sense — based on the newer meaning of tolerance. In this case, however, the right is not intolerant in the *first* sense: after all, the right is not trying to criminalize those with opposing views on these matters. On the first view of tolerance and intolerance, one must disagree with people, even vigorously, before one may tolerate them. And yet, and yet. . . . One does sometimes wonder if the rhetoric has slipped beyond vigorous, principled debate into sneering condescension that, even if it does not call for the criminalization of the opponents, so demeans and debases them that the image of iron-jawed pit bulls does not seem entirely inappropriate. Is there not *some* point at which, in the way we treat those with whom we disagree vigorously (even if we do not demand either legal sanctions against them or their enforced silence), tolerance (in the first sense) is gradually slipping over into intolerance?

These issues are tied up with some of the most debated aspects of democratic rule, the claims of majoritarianism over against the rights of individuals, and other complicated issues. We shall have occasion to think about them a little more in the last two chapters of this book. The purpose of this chapter, however, is much more modest. I merely want to document that the new tolerance, while making its claims to be free from any ethical, moral, or religious system of thought, is in fact hugely inconsistent. The problem, I shall argue, is worse than mere inconsistency in an argument: it is in fact smuggling into the culture massive structures of thought and imposing them on others who disagree, while insisting that the *others* are the intolerant people. If we were not so caught up in this situation, the ironies would be so delicious they could form the center of an interesting farcical sitcom.

On Claiming the Moral High Ground for "Tolerance"

A commonplace among those who support the new tolerance is that the enemies of tolerance are guilty of adopting strongly asserted positions. They claim to know the Truth (with a capital "T"), and that is precisely what makes them most likely to be intolerant. By contrast, the defenders of the new tolerance prefer the wisdom often ascribed to Socrates: "All I know is that I know nothing" (though Socrates never said any such thing).[2] The charge that those who claim to know the

---

2. Priscilla Sakezles, "Socratic Skepticism," www.skeptic.com/eskeptic/08-06-25.html#feature, has convincingly shown that in every instance where Socrates says things like "I do not think that I know what I do not know" he is not claiming to know

Truth are more intolerant than others can be disputed, but that is not my concern here. My concern is to show that those who claim the moral high ground of (the new) tolerance are in fact no less opinionated than those they criticize, but about other topics.

Perhaps no one has been more biting about this tendency on the left than one of the best-known writers on the left, Stanley Fish. In his 1999 book *The Trouble with Principle*,[3] Fish provides examples. For example, indigenous or Two-Thirds World peoples (for whose rights many are concerned) come out against homosexuality, and the left stumbles over how to condemn that stance without appearing to be racist or colonialist. Salman Rushdie is condemned to death under a *fatwa* issued by the Ayatollah Khomeini for writing a novel judged to be critical of Islam, and at least some on the left tut-tut that Rushdie brought it on himself by his intemperate and intolerant speech. Apparently when the principle of free speech and the principle of toleration for minorities clash, free speech must lose. Fish holds that the really dangerous element about such liberalism is that it uses the rhetoric of neutrality and elevates tolerance while not being neutral and often being intolerant. It is what Fish labels "boutique multiculturalism." But even "strong multiculturalism," which stipulates tolerance as the first principle, runs into trouble when it confronts the intolerance it loathes at the heart of another belief system. How should one respond to Muslim intolerance of Salman Rushdie? If one tolerates it, one has abandoned tolerance as a first principle; if one condemns it, one turns out to be one more boutique multiculturalist after all. In the words of another careful scholar on the left:

> For all its vaunted openness to the Other, postmodernism can be quite as exclusive and censorious as the orthodoxies it opposes. One may, by and large, speak of human culture but not human nature, gender but not class, the body but not biology, *jouissance* but not justice, post-colonialism but not the petty bourgeoisie. It is a thoroughly orthodox heterodoxy, which like any imaginary

---

that he knows nothing, still less that human knowledge is impossible. Rather, he claims not to have knowledge where in fact he does not have it (unlike most of his opponents, who claim to know what they do not know).

3. Cambridge: Harvard University Press, 1999.

form of identity needs its bogeyman and straw targets to stay in business.[4]

The examples are legion. In the name of inclusion (because, after all, we are tolerant), we may end up with exclusion (proving we are intolerant). When New York's Central Park allows New Yorkers to set up a Christian nativity scene, a Jewish menorah, and a Muslim star and crescent, each paid for by private citizens even though the displays are on public property, that's inclusion. By contrast, a few years ago when Eugene, Oregon, banned Christmas trees from public property because this would not be inclusive, they were exclusive. Under pressure, the city backed down and permitted firefighters to put up a Christmas tree on Christmas Eve and Christmas Day, but even then solemnly pronounced that if even one citizen objected the tree would have to come down. So in the name of inclusion and tolerance, the city permitted the most sensitive soul (or the greatest whiner) not only to set public policy, but to foster a policy that was intolerant of many other citizens of Eugene by a decision justifying sophomoric exclusion. During the last decade and a half, on many campuses across the country, student unions have adopted a policy that bans any student organization that does not allow its leaders to be drawn from the population of practicing homosexuals. This is of course an effort to enforce a kind of inclusion, all in the name of tolerance. The result is the decision to "derecognize" evangelical groups that as a matter of conscience cannot submit to the decree, thus excluding such groups from the campus mix. But if groups on campus cannot set their own rules for leadership of their own groups, then what is to prevent the banning of a science club because it cannot accept into its leadership a flat-earther, to ban Hillel, a Jewish campus organization, because it

---

4. Terry Eagleton, *The Illusions of Postmodernism* (Oxford: Blackwell, 1997), 26. For those interested in this probing line of inquiry, it is important to read Peter Berkowitz, "John Rawls and the Liberal Faith," *Wilson Quarterly* 26 (22 March 2002): 60-69. Berkowitz draws attention to the "faith" assumptions in Rawls's theory, assumptions regarding such values as human dignity, equality, and concern for the disadvantaged. But in articulating such foundations of liberalism, Rawls seems to vacillate between affirming that such ideas are self-evident and affirming that they rest on faith. But if the former is true, then faith is unnecessary; if faith is necessary to establish liberalism's foundations, then what exactly is the ground for criticizing the faith of others?

wants only Jews and non–Holocaust-deniers to be its leaders, or a Muslim organization because it forbids polytheist Hindus from being among its leaders? In each case, the policy could be adopted in order to enforce inclusion, and in each case the group would be excluded from the campus. In reality, of course, no student union goes so far: student unions are highly selective in their enforced inclusion. Support for homosexuals is strong; support for flat-earthers is nonexistent. But that simply shows that the student unions are *not* principled defenders of tolerance, inclusion, and free speech. Rather, they appeal to tolerance selectively in order to promote their own selective values. This is not merely accidental inconsistency; it is inconsistency with an agenda. The fact that so far the courts have largely sided with the minority student groups does not overthrow the ugliness of the policies of the student unions themselves.

According to countless Internet reports, the last decade has seen filmmaker Rob Reiner, a co-founder of Castle Rock Entertainment, come out so strongly against smoking that anyone who wants to depict smoking in a Castle Rock film must first meet with Reiner and provide a convincing justification. Reiner has repeatedly been reported to have said, "Movies are basically advertising cigarettes to kids." In other words, with the rarest of exceptions, he refuses to tolerate smoking in the films his company produces. Good on you, Rob. But why does he not take a similar stance with respect to casual sex, gratuitous violence, and blasphemous language? The defense, of course, is that Hollywood's depiction of such conduct does not *cause* similar behavior, and besides, it would be intolerant to censor the depiction of alternative ways of living. But then why does Reiner think that depicting smoking so advertises the habit that young people are induced to smoke? Why censor smoking? How is it the moral high ground to be intolerant about depicting smoking and to be tolerant about depicting gang rape?

Similar inconsistencies crop up in every domain of life. A decade ago, *First Things* reported the comments of Jewish talk show host and commentator Dennis Prager regarding developments at Duke University, which is associated with the United Methodist Church.[5] Since 1853, at the baccalaureate service Duke has given a free copy of the Bi-

5. *First Things* 111 (January 1999): 77.

ble to all participating graduates. At the end of the 1990s, Jewish faculty and students at Duke protested that it was offensive to Jewish students to be given a book that includes the New Testament. By way of response, Duke University decided that henceforth Bibles would not be given out but would be stacked in a separate room where students could go and take one if they wished. *First Things* cites Prager as follows (emphasis his):

> To summarize the situation in even simpler terms: Duke Jewish faculty and students and Jewish institutions at Duke object to Jewish students participating in a service where Duke offers a gift of a Bible *that contains their own Jewish Bible* and also the New Testament; *where any participant is free not to take that Bible;* at *a service that is entirely voluntary;* in *a university that is private* and affiliated with the Methodist Church. One of the best words to describe this attitude is actually a Hebrew/Yiddish one — chutzpah. Another word might be ingratitude. We American Jews are probably the most fortunate Jews in Jewish history. We live the freest, most economically secure lives in Jewish history in a country that not merely tolerates our religion, but has always honored it. And who made such a country possible? Men and women, nearly all of whom were Christian, who regarded Judeo-Christian values as the basis of this society, even as many of them fell short of these values. In our specific case, it was not Jews who made Duke University, it was Christians, indeed a specific Christian church. Instead of being grateful to the tradition that created their country and their university, some Duke Jewish faculty and students have decided that they are *offended* by it. . . . The Jews of Duke have undermined the Judeo-Christian and Western cultural foundations of American culture and of their university. And for what? So that Jewish students not hold a Bible containing Christian scriptures. How sad. Apparently, Multiculturalism and Tolerance don't apply to Christians.[6]

The inconsistency built into many contemporary pleas for tolerance is staggeringly obvious, even if frequently ignored. Europe, which prides itself in being much more tolerant than America, dis-

---

6. *First Things* 111 (January 1999): 77.

plays this kind of inconsistency on many fronts. When a Danish newspaper published cartoons of Muhammad and people died in the upheaval that followed, much of the discussion in the media turned on the debate between two competing values: tolerance of the new sort (Didn't the cartoonist bring this on himself, because he should have been more tolerant of Muslim feelings?) and freedom of expression (Shouldn't we preserve the freedom to publish whatever we want, even if it skewers some sacred cows?). Once again we must see that what is being advocated on the tolerance side is not the old tolerance. The old tolerance would have insisted that both Muslims and Christians have the right, indeed the obligation, to criticize the other party, including by means of satire and cartoons. The Danish cartoonists were not jeopardizing the freedom of expression of Muslims, still less their right to worship and propagate their faith. So when some Muslims responded with violence and threats of assassination, it was *they* who were being intolerant (under the old understanding of tolerance), not the publishers of the cartoons. Only by falling under the sway of the new tolerance could the charge of intolerance be attached to the cartoonist and his publisher. And meanwhile, by reducing their attachment to freedom of expression, many voices, apparently in fear because of the threats, became themselves less tolerant of those who wanted to maintain freedom of expression.

In 2006, according to the BBC,[7] a seventy-five-year-old man, Edward Atkinson, living in King's Lynn, Norwich, was waiting for a hip replacement at Queen Elizabeth Hospital. Because he is against abortion, he began mailing to the hospital pictures of aborted babies. The chief executive of the hospital, Ruth May, viewed this as a case of abuse or unacceptable behavior toward hospital staff, and cancelled the operation. Moreover, the Swaffham Magistrates Court sentenced the crippled seventy-five-year-old man to twenty-eight days in jail for "sending offensive literature" to the hospital staff. Apparently aborting a baby is legal, and one must be tolerant of abortionists — i.e., one must do nothing to offend those who perform such abortions; depicting abortion, however, is a crime, and those who distribute such depictions and oppose abortion must be jailed and refused needed health

7. Reported in *First Things* 165 (August/September 2006): 79.

care that would be provided to murderers and rapists. So here, again, is government-backed intolerance in the name of (the new) tolerance.

Does one need to point out that anti-Semitism in Europe is making a stunning and ugly comeback? The number of Jews assaulted (especially if they are wearing yarmulkes or are otherwise identifiable) and the number of synagogues defaced and occasionally destroyed are on a sweeping increase. The World Jewish Congress claims that European anti-Semitism is now the worst it has been since 1945. A few years ago a poll of nations in the European Union showed that about 60 percent of Europeans think that Israel is the greatest threat to world peace — not North Korea, not Sudan, not Iran. This has been brought about by the confluence of highly diverse sources: the far right's resurgent Nazi-style racism, the far left's political and economic anti-Semitism (Israel and America as the common enemy), and the religious hatred of Jews found among much of the growing European Muslim population. This is not to suggest that there are no other kinds of intolerance in Europe and around the world. It is merely a particularly striking instance of a culture that thinks of itself as richly tolerant (in the second sense) drifting backward toward one of the greatest intolerances (in the first sense) of the twentieth century.

On the Impact of Secularization

In the previous chapter, I argued that the processes of secularization had for many people "flipped a switch" regarding many default assumptions. Now I shall argue that many who espouse the new tolerance buy into one form or another of secularism *as if it were a neutral stance,* so that by implication those who adopt some other stance are narrow and intolerant.

Of course, scholars have created diverse trajectories of the processes of secularization. The old theory of Max Weber (1864-1920) was that secularization is the almost inexorable process in which, as modernity advances, religion retreats. That theory held broad sway until about 1970, and it is still very influential in the popular media and in many circles in Europe. Scholars in the field of sociology, however, observing how America is on many fronts simultaneously secular and religious, started speaking of "American exceptionalism" with respect to this thesis, arguing that secularization does not necessarily mean the reduction or the abolition of religion, but the squeezing of it to the periphery of life: religion becomes privatized (as we saw in the last chapter). Today it is becoming common to speak not of American exceptionalism but of European exceptionalism: America fits more comfortably into the rest of the world, where religion does not seem to be waning, while Europe is unique in the high percentage of its citizens who are agnostic or atheistic, and whose organized religions, at any rate, capture the allegiance of only a small percentage of the populace.[8] Increasingly, secularized Europeans are the only large group who think that Weber's thesis is fundamentally right.

Despite these subtleties, however, those who think of themselves as secularists, whether in Europe or America, regularly view their position as morally neutral and therefore as intrinsically superior, so that that position *ought* to be supported by law, even if it means suppressing, by law, those who contest this view. Sometimes this is put in sophisticated and elegant arguments. Writing in the *University of Chicago Law Review,* for instance, Kathleen M. Sullivan argues that the Constitution's insistence on the free exercise of religion "implies the free exercise of non-religion," which thus

> establishes a civil public order, which ends the war of all sects against all. The price of this truce is the banishment of religion from the public square, but the reward should be allowing religious subcultures to withdraw from regulation insofar as compatible with peaceful diarchic coexistence.[9]

The implications of this mandated privatization of religion Sullivan does not hesitate to spell out: "The correct baseline [for freedom of religion] is not unfettered religious liberty, but rather religious liberty in-

8. For a useful survey of these trends, see Richard John Neuhaus, "Secularizations," *First Things* 190 (February 2009): 23-28. I hasten to add that this discussion of American or European exceptionalism in the religious sphere has no *necessary* connection with the much larger debate over "American exceptionalism": see, for instance, Ted Bromund, "The Exceptional Battleground: A Controversy," *City* 4, no. 1 (2011): 46-52.

9. Kathleen M. Sullivan, "Religion and Liberal Democracy," *University of Chicago Law Review* 59 (1992): 222.

sofar as it is consistent with the establishment of the secular, moral order."[10] I fail to see how such authority assigned to the "secular, moral order" has any more limits on its gargantuan pretensions than the authority of, say, a Nazi regime or a totalitarian Communist regime.

Of course, the assumption that the secular frame of reference is the only morally neutral and therefore invariably superior stance works its way out in many fields. In the field of biblical studies, for instance, Ronald Hendel recently resigned from the Society of Biblical Literature because he became uncomfortable with the Society's willingness to tolerate evangelicals in its ranks, thereby loosening, in his view, the commitment to reason-based critical scholarship.[11] His essay shows that for him "reason" is associated with entirely naturalistic explanations of everything. The alternative lumps together "creationists, snake-handlers and faith-healers."

A more amusing example comes from Great Britain. In early 2007, Michael Portillo, a former Member of Parliament and Cabinet member, wrote:

> When last week David Cameron [then the leader of the Conservative party, and now the Prime Minister] revealed that he hopes his daughter will go to a Church of England school, his aides rushed to say that he attends Sunday worship in Kensington not as a ploy to help her chances but out of genuine religious conviction. I would be more reassured to hear that the Tory leader goes to church because that is what it takes to get a child into the best of state schools, not because he is a believer.[12]

To which R. Albert Mohler, the president of the Southern Baptist Theological Seminary, responded, "You read that right. Mr. Portillo clearly would prefer Mr. Cameron to be a hypocrite than a believer in God."[13] Mohler notes that Portillo goes on to criticize then–Prime Minister

10. Sullivan, "Religion and Liberal Democracy," 198. I am indebted to Michael Thate for drawing my attention to Sullivan's essay.

11. Ronald S. Hendel, "Farewell to SBL: Faith and Reason in Biblical Studies," *Biblical Archaeology Review* 36, no. 4 (July/August 2010): 28, 74.

12. http://www.michaelportillo.co.uk/articles/art_nipress/god.htm.

13. http://digital.library.sbts.edu/bitstream/handle/10392/1452/2007-02-26.pdf?sequence=1.

Tony Blair for the same fault of believing in God: "He is apparently serious about religion. Reportedly he takes on holiday 12th-century theological texts for poolside reading. A year ago he told us that he had prayed to God about his decision to join the American invasion of Iraq and that, since he is a believer, it is how God will judge his actions that most concerns him." This invites Mohler's riposte: "So Mr. Portillo fears a national leader who fears the judgment of God. One might think that we should instead fear the man who fears no judgment." The stunning element, of course, is the sheer hubris with which Mr. Portillo presupposes that a secular or naturalistic stance is intrinsically superior and safer. Tell that to the victims of Stalin, Mao, or Pol Pot.

The same phenomenon abounds in the political realm. When George W. Bush returned to the presidency in 2004, the most secularized opponents outdid themselves in the purple prose of indignant condescension and grating superiority.[14] One of the editors of the *American Prospect*, Robert Kuttner, criticized Democrats because they "neither warned mainstream voters of the danger of a theocratic president whose base rejects modernity nor articulated a compelling moral language of their own."[15] Apparently "modernity" will have nothing to do with God; the alternative is theocracy. Has Mr. Kuttner not read the founding fathers? Here is the same antithesis, written by Robert Reich a few months before the 2004 elections, wrapped up in Weberian presuppositions:

> The great conflict of the 21st century will not be between the West and terrorism. But terrorism is a tactic, not a belief. The true battle will be between modern civilization and anti-modernists; between those who believe in the primacy of the individual and those who believe that human beings owe their allegiance and identity to a higher authority; between those who give priority to life in this world and those who believe that human life is mere preparation for an existence beyond life; between those who believe in science, reason, and logic and those who believe that truth is revealed through Scripture and religious dogma. Terrorism will

14. See especially the detailed documentation in Ramesh Ponnuru, "Secularism and Its Discontents," *National Review* 56, no. 24 (27 December 2004): 32-35.

15. http://prospect.org/cs/articles?article=an_uncertain_trumpet_120104.

disrupt and destroy lives. But terrorism itself is not the greatest danger we face.[16]

The small element of truth in Reich's paragraph, of course, is that terrorism is not a belief but a tactic. It can be, it has been, it will be deployed by people from any number of political and religious views. What is so disconcerting about the paragraph, however, is the dogmatic lumping together of all religious people, the "anti-modernists," over against "modern civilization." More striking yet are the alignments that Garry Wills draws in his op-ed piece in the *New York Times* for 4 November 2004:

> The secular states of modern Europe do not understand the fundamentalism of the American electorate. . . . [W]e now resemble those nations less than we do our putative enemies. Where else do we find fundamentalist zeal, a rage at secularity, religious intolerance, fear of and hatred for modernity? Not in France or Britain or Germany or Italy or Spain. We find it in the Muslim world, in Al Qaeda, in Saddam Hussein's Sunni loyalists. Americans wonder that the rest of the world thinks us so dangerous, so single-minded, so impervious to international appeals. They fear jihad, no matter whose zeal is being expressed.[17]

But all religious people should no more be lumped together than all atheists or all secularists should be lumped together. Would these writers want to see themselves in the same camp as Peter Singer of Princeton University, whose atheism leads him to conclude that it would be good policy to establish a twenty-eight-day period after human birth before having the same right to life as others?

The point is that, while claiming the moral high ground, the secularists *are unambiguously attempting to push their own agendas.* They have every right to do so, of course, *but they do not have the right to assume that their stance is "neutral" and therefore intrinsically superior.* In times past, it was not uncommon for secularists (or atheists or free

16. http://prospect.org/cs/articles?articleId=7858.
17. http://www.nytimes.com/2004/11/04/opinion/04wills.html?_r=1&ex=11005 77901&ei=1&en=d52c693351bb5a97.

thinkers) to nurture a condescending tolerance toward their less-enlightened fellows. By contrast, the last decade or two witnesses to a growing hatred toward those who disagree with them. In a word, as they become more convinced of their superiority and neutrality, they become less tolerant. The problem is what John Coffey calls "the myth of secular tolerance." He writes:

> The myth is not that secular people can be tolerant, for often they are. Rather, the myth of secular tolerance is that *tolerance comes naturally to the secular person, whilst intolerance comes naturally to the religious person.* The myth suggests that simply by virtue of being secular, one is somehow immune from the temptation to vilify and persecute "the other." This is a myth in the vulgar sense that it is a commonly held belief without solid foundation; but it is also a myth in the technical sense — a moral tale that sustains and nourishes the culture and beliefs of those who hold it.[18]

On Other Agendas

With very little work, one could turn this section of the chapter into another book. Instead, I provide merely a handful of representative examples where, in organizations or movements that place a high value on the new tolerance, the evidence suggests that other agendas are at work.

(1) Several years ago I came across a thirty-two-page booklet that examined the official human rights advocacy of a number of mainline churches. Issued by the Institute on Religion and Democracy (IRD), *Human Rights Advocacy in the Mainline Protestant Churches (2000-2003)* examines the views of the United Methodist Church, the Episcopal Church, the Presbyterian Church (USA), the ELCA Lutherans, and the official documents of the National Council of Churches and the World Council of Churches. Clearly the hope of these churches was to encourage more freedom and greater tolerance. The IRD document observes, however, that during the years surveyed, there were 197 offi-

18. John Coffey, "The Myth of Secular Intolerance," *Cambridge Papers* 12, no. 3 (September 2003): 2.

cial statements from these named churches, protesting human rights abuses. Sixty-nine percent were aimed against the U.S. (37%) or Israel (32%). No criticisms were leveled against China, Libya, Syria, or North Korea, even though all four of them, on occasion, brutally deny religious freedom to their citizens. Not a single country that borders on Israel is criticized. Not for a moment am I suggesting that either America or Israel should be exempt from criticism. Yet it is impossible not to detect a pretty stifling agenda when North Korea is given a pass, despite its concentration camps where thousands die from the exhaustion of slave labor.

(2) In 2004, the Catholic League reported on their careful counting of the year-end seasonal cards published by the major greeting card companies. They counted 443 different Christmas cards, but only nine of them (2%) featured the religious significance of the festival. By contrast, of the thirty-three Hanukkah cards, twenty-six (79%) featured a Star of David or a menorah. The Kwanzaa cards were all non-religiously ethnic. Only the Christmas cards offered a "Risqué" line and a "Rude" line, featuring, among other things, sado-masochism and a nearly nude angel asking, "Ever make an angel in the snow?"; there were no Risqué or Rude Hanukkah or Kwanzaa cards. How does one explain such statistics — especially in a country that is culturally 90 percent Christian, and where close to the same percentage of the people believe that Jesus was born of a virgin? One need not postulate a nasty conspiracy theory, for conspiracy theories presuppose secret meetings and malign collusion of which there is no evidence. No, the evidence suggests something more corrosive. In the name of tolerant diversity and a free press, the agenda of hidden motives surfaces: a targeted contempt for and hatred of Christ and Christians, a contempt and hatred reserved for no other religion.[19] The current pattern of distinctly anti-Christian polemic is worse than bad taste: it betrays a myopia, not to say a willful ignorance of history, that is frankly shocking.[20]

(3) In the second chapter of this book, I gave some examples of the strange face of the new tolerance as it is found in many academic

19. For other examples in the same vein, see D. A. Carson, *Christ and Culture Revisited* (Grand Rapids: Eerdmans, 2008), 184-85.

20. Cf. Vincent Carroll and David Shiflett, *Christianity on Trial: Arguments against Anti-Religious Bigotry* (San Francisco: Encounter, 2002).

circles. Gradually more articles are appearing that chronicle the tendency of colleges to scapegoat followers of traditional religions, especially Christians and Jews.[21] One of the most penetrating (and frankly moving) testimonies I have read in this regard is Eric Miller's "Alone in the Academy."[22] Shaped by such powerful thinkers as Christopher Lasch and Christopher Shannon,[23] Miller concludes that the dominant reading of literature and history in the academy must fit the "well-traveled narrative about 'oppression' and 'freedom.'"[24] There is no other story. Other possibilities — ideological, philosophical, traditional, theological — are dismissed under the rubric "oppressor" and so cannot be tolerated. The searing iron of tolerance burns away other narratives. In the name of tolerance and freedom, the entire world becomes small and slightly lonely. Describing his own graduate studies in the 1990s, Miller goes on:

> A sure sign of our loneliness was the near-total absence of any genuine political discussion or debate within the university, whether in graduate seminars, public lectures, or less formal settings. All graduate students "knew," to take the most obvious and telling example, that "conservatism" (rarely defined or actually discussed) was pathological and thus hideous and dangerous; this assumption ended up setting the ground rules for any consideration of conservatism as either a historical subject or a contemporary point of view that might fruitfully be brought to bear on our discussions of authors, politics, and life.
>
> My gut sense was that the culture of the university didn't have the strength to accommodate any serious challenge to the dominant liberal standpoint. In this regard, Jean Bethke Elshtain's recent remark about the kind of self that has accompanied "the triumph of the therapeutic culture" is apt; it is, she says, a "quivering

21. E.g., Candace de Russy, *The Chronicle Review: The Chronicle of Higher Education* 48, no. 24 (22 February 2002), sect. 2, B11-B13.

22. *First Things* 140 (February 2004): 30-34.

23. Christopher Lasch, *The Culture of Narcissism: American Life in an Age of Diminishing Expectations* (New York: Warner, 1979); Christopher Shannon, *Conspicuous Criticism: Tradition, the Individual, and Culture in American Social Thought, from Veblen to Mills* (Baltimore: Johns Hopkins University Press, 2006).

24. Miller, "Alone in the Academy," 31.

sentimental self that gets uncomfortable very quickly, because this self has to feel good about itself all the time. Such selves do not make good arguments, they validate one another." The university in the nineties seemed a case study of this self's triumph: genuine, principled argument rarely even made an appearance there. We academics had by then become a people fighting mainly *for ourselves* — a posture that tends to foster, with some rapidity, a defensive, emotional state of mind, not one centered on open-mindedness, rationality, and all the other attributes that intellectuals are supposed to possess.[25]

Miller, who now teaches at a Christian liberal arts college, is quick to confess that Christian colleges, despite substantive differences in belief and behavior with those of their secular equivalents, often trip over the same narrowness, constrained by this "globalizing, homogenizing age" — wondering "if our own halfway covenant with modernity is not, in the end, a devil's bargain"[26] — even while he insists there is no responsible choice but to press on toward more robust thought.

(4) The wonderful world of politics throws up no end of examples where in the name of tolerance some other agenda is smuggled in. In the American city that most wants to be known for its tolerance, namely, San Francisco, 25,000 Christian teenagers gathered in 2006 to rally against what they called popular culture's "terrorism against virtue." The city's supervisors passed resolutions warning against their malign influence, and some of the Assemblymen were apoplectic. One of them was widely quoted as saying these teens were "loud, they're obnoxious, they're disgusting, and they should get out of San Francisco."[27] Mercifully, the *San Francisco Chronicle* commented on the irony: "the supervisors' reaction was so boorishly over the top that only one word could describe it: Intolerant."[28]

25. Miller, "Alone in the Academy," 31-32.
26. Miller, "Alone in the Academy," 34.
27. E.g., *SFGate,* as reported in http://articles.sfgate.com/2006-03-25/news/17286242_1_culture-war-battle-cry-popular-culture.
28. http://articles.sfgate.com/2006-03-28/opinion/17286464_1_supervisors-christian-battle-cry.

*   *   *

But enough. The main point of this chapter is to observe how the new tolerance thinks of itself as intrinsically neutral, free from any ethical, moral, or religious system of thought, yet this is not so. The problem is worse than mere inconsistency, for the new tolerance regularly smuggles into the culture massive structures of thought and imposes them on others who disagree, while insisting that the *others* are the intolerant people.

FIVE

The Church and Christian Truth Claims

The Challenges

The Charge of Intolerance

In his 1991 book *The Good Society,* Robert Bellah quotes a recent graduate from Harvard, speaking on his graduation day: "Among my classmates, however, I believe that there is one idea, one sentiment, which we have all acquired at some point in our Harvard careers; and that, ladies and gentlemen, is, in a word, confusion." A graduate student at the same commencement declared,

> They tell us it's heresy to suggest the superiority of some value, fantasy to believe in moral argument, slavery to submit to a judgment sounder than your own. The freedom of our day is the freedom to devote yourself to any values we please, on the mere condition that we do not believe them to be true.[1]

The problem is bound up with what I have called the new tolerance. In the name of refusing to say that some positions are wrong, this tolerance becomes a synonym for ethical or religious neutrality. It

---

1. Robert Bellah, *The Good Society* (New York: Knopf, 1991), 43-44; quote also in Steven Garber, *The Fabric of Faithfulness* (Downers Grove: InterVarsity, 2007), 222. I am grateful to Tom Frakes for drawing my attention to this quotation.

refuses to adjudicate among competing truth claims and moral claims on the ground that to do so would be intolerant. By contrast, the older tolerance — what J. Budziszewski calls "true tolerance"[2] — actually *requires* you to take a stand among the competing truth and ethical claims, for otherwise you are not in a position to put up with something with which you disagree. Part of the crises we face in domains as diverse as education, politics, and law, not to mention religion, springs from the decline of the old tolerance and the triumph of the new. For the sad reality is that ethical neutrality — this new tolerance — is finally impossible, but as long as it is pursued it cripples policy choices and abolishes principled choices because it has banished the framework of truth and morality on which true tolerance depends. In this chapter I reflect primarily on truth, and in the next, on morality.

Neither the old tolerance nor the new is an intellectual position; rather, each is a social response. The *old* tolerance is the willingness to put up with, allow, or endure people and ideas with whom we disagree; in its purest form, the *new* tolerance is the social commitment to treat all ideas and people as equally right, save for those people who disagree with this view of tolerance. Advocates of the new tolerance sacrifice wisdom and principle in support of just one supreme good: upholding their view of tolerance. So those who uphold and practice the older tolerance, enmeshed as they inevitably are in some value system, are written off as intolerant. Thus banished, they no longer deserve a place at the table.

Nowhere is this conflict deeper than in the competing views of religion in general and of Christianity in particular. The best minds on both sides of the debate recognize that the heart of the issue is truth. Stanley Fish, who for many years chaired the English department at Duke University and then taught at the University of Illinois and subsequently became the Davidson-Kahn Distinguished University Professor of Humanities and Law at Florida International University, is no friend of confessional Christianity, but he sees the issue more clearly than some who call themselves Christians. One of the

2. J. Budziszewski, *True Tolerance: Liberalism and the Necessity of Judgment* (New Brunswick: Transaction, 2000).

most articulate defenders of a strong form of postmodernism, he nevertheless recognizes that those who want to teach the Bible as literature in the public schools while bracketing the question of truth preserve their postmodern credentials, but sacrifice the Bible for what it claims to be, for what Christians claim it to be.

> The truth claims of a religion — at least of religions like Christianity, Judaism and Islam — are not incidental to its identity; they *are* its identity.
>
> The metaphor that theologians use to make the point is the shell and the kernel: ceremonies, parables, traditions, holidays, pilgrimages — these are merely the outward signs of something that is believed to be informing them and giving them significance. That something is the religion's truth claims. Take them away and all you have is an empty shell, an ancient video game starring a robed superhero who parts the waters of the Red Sea, followed by another who brings people back from the dead. I can see the promo now: more exciting than "Pirates of the Caribbean" or "The Matrix." That will teach, but you won't be teaching religion.
>
> The difference between the truth claims of religion and the truth claims of other academic topics lies in the penalty for getting it wrong. A student or a teacher who comes up with the wrong answer to a crucial question in sociology or chemistry might get a bad grade or, at the worst, fail to be promoted. Those are real risks, but they are nothing to the risk of being mistaken about the identity of the one true God and the appropriate ways to worship him (or her). Get that one wrong, and you don't lose your grade or your job, you lose your salvation and get condemned to an eternity in hell.
>
> Of course, the "one true God" stuff is what the secular project runs away from, or "brackets." It counsels respect for all religions and calls upon us to celebrate their diversity. But religion's truth claims don't want your respect. They want your belief and, finally, your soul. They are jealous claims. Thou shalt have no other God before me.[3]

3. The original essay, "Religion without Truth," was published as an op-ed piece in the *New York Times* for 31 March 2007 (now available at http://www.nytimes.com/

A similar point has been made by (then) Joseph Cardinal Ratzinger (now Pope Benedict XVI): if the truth question is ruled inappropriate in the realm of religion and belief, then the status of religion and of belief is itself transmuted into something that no believer recognizes.[4]

Many contemporary voices deny that religion has much to do with truth that can be defended in the public square. This suspicion regarding the place of truth in religion is related to one of the most central myths of our time. In one of his essays, Phil Miles nicely outlines it for us.[5] According to this myth, a society is likely to be most tolerant if it holds to flexible, non-dogmatic, even multivalent notions of truth; conversely, a society is likely to be most *in*tolerant where it holds to absolute truths, truths that are inflexible, unbending. In other words, tyranny and tolerance find themselves in a perennial battle, and which pole triumphs is tied largely to the conception of truth that we sustain.

But does this myth capture reality? Is the myth true? Miles sets forth his thesis: "The reality of the situation is just the *opposite* of what we have been led to believe. Put simply, tyranny is not the inevitable outcome of an absolutist view of truth, but is, rather, the direct product of *relativism*. Likewise, tolerance arises not from relativism but from the very thing that our society anathematizes — the belief in absolutes."[6]

It would take too long to lay out the details of Miles's argument. Suffice it to say that he holds that many of our categories for thinking about these things are inappropriate. In part, he argues by case study. He begins with Japan, a country where he lived for many years. In most Western cultures, we live in the shadow of the Enlightenment, which taught us to classify our experience into two categories: the one, full of non-absolutes, is characterized by emotion, aesthetics, the arts; the other is characterized by absolutes, objectivity, science, logical thought, and truth. These two categories are mutually exclusive.

2007/03/31/opinion/31fishs.html). A follow-up piece appeared on 15 April 2007 (see http://opinionator.blogs.nytimes.com/2007/04/15/religion-without-truth-part-two/).

4. Joseph Ratzinger, *Truth and Tolerance: Christian Belief and World Religions* (San Francisco: Ignatius, 2004).

5. Phil Miles, "Of Truth, Tolerance and Tyranny," *kategoria* 22 (2001): 7-27.

6. Miles, "Of Truth, Tolerance and Tyranny," 8.

The second category is the domain of both tyranny and objective truth. By contrast, Japan brings the two categories together in ways that would be judged incompatible in most of the Western world: on the one hand, haiku poetry and delicate paintings of enchanting cherry blossoms, and on the other, ruthless business corporations and political machinations. The fact that these two categories coexist and interpenetrate each other in Japan is part of what makes Japan seem so "mysterious" to the Western observer. In reality, Miles argues, what is often called the "iron triangle" — "the triad of elected government, big business and the bureaucracy"[7] — exerts enormous power in a frankly oppressive manner. "There is no need to picture this in terms of dictators and jack-boots. Things are done a lot more subtly in Japan, but the salient fact is that those who hold power use it to control the lives of those beneath them."[8] There is little tradition of elected officials being "servants of the people"; in fact, the people exist to serve the state and culture, not to mention the company to which a person belongs. In Japanese culture, there is little notion of "right" and "wrong" in absolute terms; it is well known that there is no Japanese word for "sin." In this sense, Japanese society is relativistic — i.e., what is "right" depends on the situation in which you find yourself, determined by the social expectations of your position in the power structure. Miles writes,

> Japanese are very adept at assessing what is required in a situation and acting accordingly. This is often misunderstood by Westerners as duplicity, but it is simply the way life must be lived where all is relative. Truth itself becomes merely a social construct. If everybody believes something to be true, or if the powers that be say that it is, then for the practical purposes of daily life, it is true. As the Japanese say, it's safe to cross against a red light if everyone does it together.[9]

In other words, Japan is a case study in which a kind of relativism opens up the door to a kind of social tyranny that massively discounts

7. Miles, "Of Truth, Tolerance and Tyranny," 11.
8. Miles, "Of Truth, Tolerance and Tyranny," 11.
9. Miles, "Of Truth, Tolerance and Tyranny," 11-12.

the significance of the individual and therefore squashes individualism. Miles argues that in this sort of culture, if there were, say, unambiguous and objective moral law to which *individuals* could appeal, there could be a critique of the unfettered deployment of social and political power. It is the *absence* of such objective standards that makes the oppressiveness of the culture possible.

Though it is no part of Miles's argument, one might observe that in the twentieth century the greatest political crushing of individualism occurred under Marxism and Fascism. Both deployed not only brute force but also massive propaganda machines to keep people safely in line with the party dogma. Truth was what Joseph Goebbels (for instance) said it was.

In the light of such case studies, one becomes aware that individualism that can become socially destructive (everyone does that which is right in their own eyes) may, in this broken world, alternatively serve as a bulwark standing athwart massive social and political tyrannies crying, "Enough!" *But it is hard to see whence the moral fortitude for such a stance will come if we systemically lose the category of objective truth.* Martyrs are not made of sponge.[10]

Another central myth of our time is that God is infinitely tolerant, that Jesus is infinitely tolerant. There is of course a smidgeon of truth in such assertions. Despite his unlimited power and untarnished holiness, the tolerance of God is displayed in his forbearance with sinners (Romans 3:25; Acts 17:30). He might be expected to provide instant justice, but instead he is long-suffering (to resurrect a word that has largely gone out of use), longing for our repentance (Romans 2:1-4). Scripture repeatedly says he is "slow to anger" (e.g., Exodus 34:6). He is so much more forbearing than his own people are that sometimes they are driven to question his justice (Habakkuk 1:2-4, 13). Nevertheless God's forbearance is not infinite. Scripture also declares that "he does not leave the guilty unpunished" (Exodus 34:7). The Bible anticipates the coming of a day of wrath "when God judges people's secrets through Jesus Christ" (Romans 2:16; cf. Acts 17:31;

10. Some of the preceding paragraphs first appeared in D. A. Carson, "Editorial: Contrarian Reflections on Individualism," *Themelios* 35 (2010): 378-83, http://www.thegospelcoalition.org/publications/35-3/editorial-contrarian-reflections-on-individualism.

Revelation 14:18; 19:1-3; 21:8). More important yet: God is better than tolerant. He does not merely put up with our sin and anarchy; rather, he is unimaginably kind and loving, demonstrated most overwhelmingly in the fact that he has sent his Son to pay the price of our sinfulness and restore us to himself. To talk about the tolerance of God apart from this richer biblical portrayal of God is to do him an injustice. His love is better than tolerance; his wrath guarantees justice that mere tolerance can never imagine.

Similarly with respect to Jesus. On the one hand, Jesus did say, "Do not judge, or you too will be judged" (Matthew 7:1) — though the biblically illiterate claim that this frowns on all attempts at moral discernment (though the verse occurs in the Sermon on the Mount, which abounds in moral distinctions) and prohibits making any moral judgments about others (though the same chapter presents Jesus as the supreme Judge [7:21-23] and requires that his followers make distinctions in people too [7:6]), paying no attention either to the immediate context or to the dominant emphases in Jesus' life. In its context, this much-quoted passage condemns judgmentalism — a self-righteous condemnation of others — not humble and moral alignment with what God himself graciously discloses. Still, Jesus was known to befriend public sinners, to weep over the city of Jerusalem for its blindness, to pray for the forgiveness of those who crucified him, and to demand that his followers love their enemies. On the other hand, this is not the entire biblical portrait. He speaks more of hell than does anyone else in the Bible, and he insists that he himself is the only way to the Father (John 14:6). In one chapter alone he declares six times, "Woe to you, teachers of the law and Pharisees, you hypocrites!" (Matthew 23), declaring that they are "blind men" and a "brood of vipers" (23:19, 33). Small wonder the late Colin Gunton could write, "The value of such passages . . . is to show that he was not a tolerant man. And yet the means of its expression was from beginning to end unrepressive, even to the cross. That may be part of the cost the church will pay for following that lead in the repressive postmodern world."[11]

---

11. Colin Gunton, "Revelation: Do Christians Know Something No One Else Knows?" in *Tolerance and Truth: The Spirit of the Age or the Spirit of Christ?* ed. Angus

Inside the Church

One might have thought that the broad cultural triumph of (the new) tolerance would be limited in reach: it would dictate what is acceptable in the culture at large, but would not presume to reshape every private enclave within the culture. After all, if this new tolerance can be enforced in the culture at large, there is little need to seek similar control within private institutions or within churches or denominations. These private groupings can proceed on their benighted way without threat to the broader culture.

Increasingly, however, that is precisely what is *not* happening. Especially when churches take a moral stance that runs counter to the dominant stance adopted by the media, the media feel no qualms about attacking the churches for their intolerance. For instance, in recent years we have witnessed a number of prominent Roman Catholic politicians claiming that while they are personally against abortion, they think they should vote to support "pro-choice" rather than "pro-life." After all, they say, they are merely observing the separation of church and state. When some Catholic bishops then announce that such persons will in their dioceses be barred from receiving Communion, the media become apoplectic. Not only are these churches breaking down the separation of church and state, but they are massively intolerant — the ultimate sin in the media's catalog of vices.

A raft of issues calls for reflection. Are not the media proving intolerant of the churches that they judge to be intolerant? Does not any church, as a private organization, have the right to discipline its own in line with its declared beliefs and policies? Only the most amazingly narrow reading of history warrants the view that citizens with moral values grounded in religious beliefs are forbidden to articulate those beliefs and vote for those values. One recalls the well-known speech by President Abraham Lincoln in which he commented scathingly on those who declared that they were personally against slavery even while insisting that they would not want slavery to be denounced as wrong:

Morrison, Edinburgh Dogmatics Conference Papers (Edinburgh: Rutherford House, 2007), 19. At a more popular level, see John MacArthur, *The Jesus You Can't Ignore: What You Must Learn from the Bold Confrontations of Christ* (Nashville: Thomas Nelson, 2010).

But those who say they hate slavery, and are opposed to it, . . . where are they? Let us apply a few tests. You say that you think slavery is wrong, but you denounce all attempts to restrain it. Is there anything else you think wrong, that you are not willing to deal with as a wrong? Why are you so careful, so tender of this wrong and no other? You will not let us *do* a single thing as if it was wrong; there is no place where you will allow it to be even *called* wrong! We must not call it wrong in the Free States, because it is *not* there, and we must not call it wrong in the Slave States because it *is* there; we must not call it wrong in politics because that is bringing morality into politics, and we must not call it wrong in the pulpit because that is bringing politics into religion . . . and there is no single place, according to you, where a wrong thing can be called a wrong thing![12]

Church leaders who uphold the discipline of their churches are not only doing their jobs; they are following the instruction and example of the New Testament. The exalted Christ criticizes the church in Thyatira for tolerating false prophet Jezebel, in particular her teaching and immorality (Revelation 2:20). Elsewhere Paul wants a church member who has fallen into grievous sexual sin, and who will not repent, to be removed from the congregation (1 Corinthians 5). He expects the same congregation to discipline certain of its teachers for preaching "another Jesus" (2 Corinthians 10-13). If there is any commitment to adhere to biblical standards and mandates, not least the teaching of Jesus, this seems a wiser course than that advocated by one respondent to *Time:* "Wow, it's been 2,000 years, and the Catholic Church still doesn't understand Jesus. The bishops should keep in mind that Jesus preached tolerance toward all. Everyone was invited to his dinner."[13] "Tolerance toward all"? Certainly everyone is invited to the messianic banquet, but they are expected to wear the robes of repentance and faith issuing in obedience. This Jesus says, "Not everyone who says to me, 'Lord, Lord,' will enter the kingdom of heaven, but only those who do the will of my Father who is in heaven. Many

12. Abraham Lincoln, "Speech at New Haven, Connecticut [1860]," in *Lincoln: Speeches and Writings, 1859-1865* (New York: Library of America, 1989), 140-41.

13. *Time* 163, no. 25 (21 June 2004).

will say to me on that day, 'Lord, Lord, did we not prophesy in your name and in your name drive out demons and in your name perform many miracles?' Then I will tell them plainly, 'I never knew you. Away from me, you evildoers!'" (Matthew 7:21-23). Moreover, on some matters the New Testament distinguishes between the level of tolerance expected within the church and within the broader culture:

> I wrote to you in my letter not to associate with sexually immoral people — not at all meaning the people of this world who are immoral, or the greedy and swindlers, or idolaters. In that case you would have to leave this world. But now I am writing to you that you must not associate with anyone who claims to be a brother or sister but is sexually immoral or greedy, an idolater or slanderer, a drunkard or swindler. Do not even eat with such people.
>
> What business is it of mine to judge those outside the church? Are you not to judge those inside? God will judge those outside. "Expel the wicked person from among you." (1 Corinthians 5:9-13)

More striking is the fact that the media are prone to condemn churches for their intolerance even when the issue is not a moral stance that conflicts with public agendas, but a purely doctrinal matter of immediate intrinsic importance only to the church. Consider the visit of Episcopal Bishop John Spong to Australia. In his native America, Spong has built a career on denying virtually every central doctrine of the Christian faith. He has strenuously denied the virgin birth of Jesus, the deity of Christ, that Joseph ever existed, that God is a personal being, that Jesus (or anyone else) ever performed miracles, that Jesus died for our sins, that he was raised from the dead, and so forth. He has affirmed that the doctrine of penal substitution is akin to divine child abuse, and suggested that the apostle Paul was a repressed homosexual. The Anglican Primate of Australia, Archbishop John Aspinall, belongs to that wing of Australian Anglicanism that vies with Spong for the number of Christian doctrines it can find to deny, so it was scarcely surprising when he invited Spong, in 2007, to deliver two sermons in Brisbane's St. John's Cathedral. By contrast, Sydney's Archbishop Peter Jensen, a confessional evangelical, refused to allow Spong to speak under Anglican auspices anywhere in the Sydney diocese. When the media picked up on the debate, guess which archbishop they labeled tolerant and which they gleefully denounced as intolerant — even though what Jensen was doing was protecting his flock from the systematic attempt to undermine a confessional stance that goes back two thousand years, a stance that bishops are sworn to uphold?

Three years earlier, the Episcopal Bishop of Virginia, Peter J. Lee, was widely reported to have defended his liberal vote in the General Convention — a vote to overturn a moral stance clearly taught in the Bible and long upheld by Christians everywhere — by saying, "If you must make a choice between heresy and schism, always choose heresy. For as a heretic you are only guilty of a wrong opinion. As a schismatic, you have torn and divided the body of Christ. Choose heresy every time."[14] Apparently most of the assembly applauded. We can only conclude that Bishop Lee does not establish his priorities in the light of Scripture. We have already seen that Christ himself can berate a church for being too tolerant of false teaching (Revelation 2:20, mentioned above). We must also ask if we are truly dealing with "the body of Christ" when people claim to be Christians but have no intention of submitting to the Lordship of King Jesus. It sounds more like an awkward union between genuine believers and those with not much more than an aesthetic and sentimental attachment to an institution called the church, divorced from revealed and mandated truth joyfully believed, confessed, and obeyed. That sort of unity is nowhere in Scripture held up as something to be admired or pursued.

Of course, some schisms are indefensible, the results of petty squabbles and powerful personalities with egos the size of small planets. Yet that is rather different from saying that in a contest between heresy and schism one must always choose the former.

The Subtle Pressure to Dumb Down, Dilute, and Minimize the Gospel

During the dark days of the Balkan conflict and its accompanying genocide, the *New York Times* ran an editorial reflecting on how each

---

14. The matter has been widely reported: e.g., http://www.layman.org/ News.aspx?article=14149; Richard John Neuhaus in *First Things* 142 (April 2004): 60.

of the three great monotheistic religions celebrates a religious festival at about the same time: Judaism celebrates Passover, Christianity celebrates Easter, and Islam celebrates Id al-Adha. The editorial is worth quoting at length:

> But if solace can be drawn in the coincidence of these days of prayer, it is in the lesson of how much these religions have in common at a time when so many of their adherents are in conflict.
>
> Passover celebrates the emergence of the Jewish people, but its universal drama is that of an escape from oppression, a declaration of freedom and self-determination that remains at issue 3,500 years after it was first heard. The ancient Hebrews' exodus from Egypt clears the way for them to receive a code of conduct from one God, a code that defines what forever makes them Jews. But this week as Jews eat matzoh at Passover, the "bread of affliction" can symbolize not simply the flight from Egypt, but the constant danger of regarding any people as strangers in their own land. It is no accident that the Passover seder has in recent years drawn the faithful from other religions and backgrounds. Alienation and expulsion, after all, is the oldest and perhaps most shocking of human dramas. The tragedy in the Balkans now is that there is no sign yet of any promise of return or deliverance, but the deep yearning for that promise is surely what can lead to action by others.
>
> The universal symbolism of Easter, which Orthodox Christians celebrate April 11, is about a promise of salvation after defeat that is of a deeply personal nature, rather than the emergence of a people. For Christians and non-Christians alike, the story Easter celebrates is that of one man maintaining his faithfulness before the military might of an oppressive government and the taunts of the crowd, a lesson of integrity and determination that has molded much of civilization as we know it. This story of sacrifice and redemption does little, of course, to lessen the pain in Kosovo. But its vision of justice rising above the temporal powers of the day is a reminder that the human spirit can triumph in the end.
>
> The Muslim holiday of Id al-Adha may be less familiar to most Americans, but it too is about regeneration and is observed by a vast multitude of people, including in this instance most of the

victims of the "ethnic cleansing" in Kosovo. It is a festival of sacrifice and the annual pilgrimage to Mecca. As Muslims see fellow Muslims forced from an inhospitable place in search of a place that will receive them, they cannot help but think this week of Mohammed's persecution and flight from Mecca to Medina, where he was welcomed and where he built his faith. The holiday also commemorates Abraham's sacrifice of the ram as a substitute for his son, with its echoes of the paschal lamb of Passover and the lamb of God of Christianity.

Some have characterized the war in the Balkans as an ancient implacable conflict among religions. But in fact, it is testimony to the ability of ruthless leaders to persecute others in the name of religion, ignoring the genuine tradition of tolerance enshrined in Judaism, Christianity and Islam and articulated by the prophets, saints and seers of each faith.[15]

Oh, dear. The three festivals have been recast into sentimental twaddle. The supernatural has been stripped out; anything distinctive has been reinterpreted in personal and psychological terms. Instead of the exodus being the liberation of God's uniquely loved covenant people by the living God himself, it is now a "universal drama" about "escape from oppression, a declaration of freedom and self-determination." Moses would be surprised to learn he was leading the people into self-determination. The Passover is about alienation and expulsion; no mention is made of the Passover lamb whose blood, sprinkled on the doorposts and lintel, ensures that the angel of destruction passes over the family that has put its confidence in the blood of the lamb, in line with the promises of God. Easter is "about a promise of salvation after defeat that is of a deeply personal nature, rather than the emergence of a people": so much for the church for which the Christ of Easter shed his blood. It's really about one man standing against military oppression and "a reminder that the human spirit can triumph in the end." Precisely what kind of reading leaps from an empty tomb and the biblical resurrection appearances to a generalized triumph of the human spirit? And to suggest that the commemoration of Abraham's sacrifice

15. "A Season of Sacrifice," the *New York Times,* 4 April 1999 (can be accessed now at http://www.nytimes.com/1999/04/04/opinion/a-season-of-sacrifice.html).

in Islam has "echoes of the paschal lamb of Passover and the lamb of God of Christianity" would throw pious Muslims into paroxysms of derisive laughter. Quite apart from the fact that an event that occurs *before* two other events can scarcely be said to have *echoes* of those events (anticipatory foreshadowings, perhaps, but not echoes), in Muslim thought Abraham's action signals his willingness to sacrifice, at Allah's command, what he most cherished, nothing more. The theological themes bound up with Passover are entirely alien to Muslim thought, and the notion that Jesus is the lamb that takes away the sin of the world is regarded as superstition. Muhammad's piety "terminated the need for animal sacrifice," so that the slaughter of animals in today's Mecca celebrations are to provide food for the poor.[16]

Of course, what the op-ed piece in the *New York Times* wanted was to turn observant Jews, Christians, and Muslims into nice, tame, theological liberals. If that argument had been made on its own terms, one could engage in serious discussion. But to argue that this is what the three respective religious festivals *really* mean is laughable.

Or consider media reports of the horrific martyrdom of a Christian missionary and his two sons, who were burned to death in 1999 in northern India. The story got more traction in the press than usual because the missionary, Graham Staines, and his wife ran a leper colony. I have no idea what the balance of his mission was, but not a few media outlets gave the impression that moral indignation at his death is acceptable because he was serving lepers and not "proselytizing." Would it have been acceptable to burn the man and his sons to death if he had also been preaching the gospel of God's great love in Christ Jesus?

The deeper tragedy, however, is that many Christians, cowed perhaps by such presentations, are tempted to depict their faith in similarly secular terms. The substance of what the Bible says becomes domesticated. Instead of bearing witness to the gospel, which joyfully announces God's rescue plan and shows how it is intimately tied to the person and work of Jesus Christ, we begin to feel it is more important to show we are nice and compassionate. What is lost, of course, is

16. See, for instance, Shabbir Akhtar, *Islam as Political Religion: The Future of an Imperial Faith* (London: Routledge, 2011), 75.

the simple truth. All of this springs from a widespread cultural intoxication with the new tolerance.

Aspects of Christian Truth Claims

In this section I cannot hope to outline the structure of Christian truth. Rather, my aim is to unpack some of the ways in which Christians who attempt to be faithful to the Bible are bound to uphold certain truths — truths that remain true whether anyone believes them or not, truths that are bound up with the gospel, truths that cannot be sacrificed on the altar of the great goddess of relativism. And then I close the chapter by arguing that none of this makes Christians intolerant in the old sense of that word. If they are judged intolerant in the new sense, the price of escaping the charge is too high to pay: it would mean abandoning Christ.

The following points are suggestive, not exhaustive.

Truth Grounded in Revelation   That revelation has come to us in the natural world, in great events of miraculous power attested by witnesses, in the personal work of the Spirit of God, in the enormously rich variety of writings that make up the Bible, and supremely in the person of Jesus Christ. These are not mutually exclusive channels. For instance, most of what we know propositionally about Jesus is found in the Bible, including those parts that preserve the testimony of witnesses — so here we have Jesus himself, witnesses who have left words about him, and the Bible that preserves them and conveys them.

Three things must be said about this content.

First, the content can be — indeed, has been — put into propositions, creeds, catechisms, statements of faith. It has substance. Of course, there is an interpretive element in all our confessions, for finite beings cannot know anything without interpreting it. Only Omniscience can escape the limitations of perspectivalism — of looking at things from a limited perspective. But that does not mean that all perspectives are equally valid, or that there is no truth in any particular interpretation. Moreover, especially when the Bible treats certain topics again and again, we can know certain things about those topics truly. As Christians band together to study the Bible, they come to convictions about what the Bible is saying — and that leads, rightly, to shared creeds that are modifiable only by more light from the Bible itself. Our confession of such truth cannot participate in the perfection of Omniscience, but it is nonetheless valid and appropriate to the limitations of our finitude and our fallenness. Better yet, it is made possible by a gracious God who condescends to disclose himself in human words, and by the Spirit who convicts rebels of sin and illumines darkened minds. The substance can be summarized in a few lines, in lengthy treatises, or anything in between. It will include many wonderful truths about God, including his perfections, his holiness, his personhood, his omniscience, omnipresence, and omnipotence, the triunity of his being, the faithfulness of his ways, the graciousness of his pursuit of his rebellious image-bearers; the doctrines of creation and fall; the history of Abraham, of Israel, of the Abrahamic and Mosaic covenants; the rise of the Davidic monarchy with its attendant promises; the coming of Jesus, virgin-born, truly God and truly human being; his perfect life and matchless teaching, his propitiating and expiating death, his triumphant resurrection displaying his vindication before his Father and his triumph over Satan and his demonic hosts; the gift of the Holy Spirit poured out on God's elect, both the seal of God's ownership of these people and the down payment of the inheritance yet to come; Christ's multi-faceted kingdom that is already forcefully advancing in this dark world but that will reach consummation in the splendor of the new heaven and the new earth, the home of righteousness, where Jesus' blood-bought people, the church drawn from every tribe and nation, will enjoy resurrection existence and the bliss of love and holiness forever. The only alternative is hell itself. Nor can we ignore the many biblical claims to the exclusiveness of Jesus as the way to be reconciled to the one God, the God who made us, who redeems us, and who will be our Judge on the last day.

There is *substance* in Christian confessionalism.

Second, this substance is more than social-linguistic convention, the stuff of widely held popular beliefs *that do not actually refer to anything outside the beliefs.* This substance is *out there.* It is true, or false, *in that sense.* Stanley Fish, in the lengthy quotation cited earlier in this chapter, has it exactly right. We are not saved by beliefs about God, Christ, the cross, and so forth, *regardless of whether such beliefs are validated by the truthfulness of what is believed.* In that sense, we are saved by Christ, not by beliefs about Christ *regardless of whether Christ actually ever existed.*

Third, the substance is not designed to feed a utilitarian narcissism. A quarter of a century ago, Neil Postman reminded us, "I believe I am not mistaken in saying that Christianity is a demanding and serious religion. When it is delivered as easy and amusing, it is another kind of religion altogether."[17] The more recent study by Jean M. Twenge and W. Keith Campbell, *The Narcissism Epidemic,*[18] offers ample evidence as to how widespread is this domestication of religion, not least forms of Christianity, to the service of self — or, more precisely, to the service of self's most narcissistic instincts. With our bookstores sporting best-selling titles such as *Become a Better You, Maximize the Moment: God's Action Plan for Your Life, Your Best Life Now,* and *It's Your Time,* it is not surprising, though more than a little disappointing, to find many preachers and commentators succumbing to the same urges. In one of his essays, Shane Rosenthal draws attention to the following introduction to the book of Ezra:

> Who are you? I'm a sports fan. I'm the child of a politician. I'm a guitar player. I'm a teenager. I'm a CPA. I'm Asian. I'm Methodist. I'm in the top tax bracket. Sometimes we identify ourselves through our interests. Other times we identify ourselves according to age, ethnic background, or income. Sometimes we identify ourselves through our professions, or our professions of faith. So who are you anyway? That's the central question of the book of Ezra.[19]

Does any thoughtful reader seriously think that Ezra is primarily interested in helping his readers establish appropriate identities, that this is the "central question" of the book? Even allowing some license

---

17. *Amusing Ourselves to Death: Public Discourse in the Age of Show Business* (New York: Penguin, 1985), 121.

18. New York: Free Press, 2009.

19. Shane Rosenthal, "Reflecting upon Scripture: 'You're So Vain, You Probably Think This Text Is about You,'" *Modern Reformation* 19, no. 5 (2010): 24, citing *TNIV Audio Bible* (Grand Rapids: Zondervan, 2005).

of homiletical application, this is, at best, of the most marginal interest to Ezra.

Two sociologists have given us the category "Moralistic Therapeutic Deism," which, they say, largely dominates the religious life of American young people from a wide variety of religious affiliations.[20] I suspect that MTD, as it is called, captures a much wider span of ages than youth alone. The five tenets of MTD are:

(1) A God exists who created and orders the world and watches over human life on earth.
(2) God wants people to be good, nice, fair to each other, as taught in the Bible and by most world religions.
(3) The central goal of life is to be happy and to feel good about oneself.
(4) God does not need to be particularly involved in one's life except when God is needed to resolve a problem.
(5) Good people go to heaven when they die.

In other words, utilitarian narcissism reigns triumphant: God exists, but only to make us happy and nice, which is the aim of existence. Otherwise God minds his own business. That's how I read the Bible, and who are you to say something different?

By contrast, the truth of the Bible, as we have seen, focuses on our rebellion and need as God sees them, and on God as the ruler, sovereign, judge, and gracious Savior who alone can rescue us from our sin and reconcile us to himself. These things can be tested by the systematic study of Scripture. Those who hold, for instance, to MTD, or to the essential equivalence of all religions, simply cannot make their case out of any holistic reading of the Bible, but only by the most egregious and subjective proof-texting.

Truth Tied to Early Christian History My focus here is not the history found within the New Testament documents (as important as that

---

20. Christian Smith and Melinda Lundquist Denton, *Soul Searching: The Religious and Spiritual Lives of American Teenagers* (New York: Oxford University Press, 2005).

subject is), but the history of the ensuing years. For during the last decade and a half a number of writers with media savvy have unleashed books and articles to support the view that originally Christianity was pluralistic in content and largely tolerant (in the new sense!) in attitude. There was no agreed orthodoxy, but highly diverse theological syntheses. We catch glimpses of the complexities, it is argued, when we peruse the many apocryphal gospels and other writings that never made it into the New Testament canon — books with titles such as *Gospel of Thomas, Gospel of Peter,* and so forth.[21] Unfortunately, we are told, what became "orthodoxy" won out and opposed every view other than that of orthodoxy. Our New Testament canon is such a late development, it is argued; in the first couple of centuries there was much more diversity. If the fourth- and fifth-century church councils formulated creeds still recited today, they did so at the expense of shutting down everyone else. So Elaine Pagels promotes *The Gnostic Gospels,*[22] which, she claims, advocated tolerance and promoted egalitarianism, while Bart Ehrman bemoans *Lost Christianities.*[23]

The subtext of these and similar books is that originally Christianity was diverse *and tolerant.* Sadly, relatively late orthodoxy made it narrow, bigoted, hate-filled, and intolerant. So don't trust people who talk about orthodoxy. Surely we are in a much better situation today, Ehrman argues, when Western culture is much more akin to the "famous tolerance" of Roman paganism. Of course, the Romans were not very tolerant of the proto-orthodox, sometimes going on persecution sprees and killing quite a lot of them. But it was the Christians' own fault for being intolerant.[24]

As popular as this view has become, it is historical nonsense. Even a casual reading of the New Testament discloses how many of its writers were concerned to maintain the truth of the gospel (e.g.,

---

21. These can most conveniently be read in English in Wilhelm Schneemelcher, ed., *New Testament Apocrypha,* 2nd ed., 2 vols. (Cambridge: James Clarke, 1991-92). To this one should add James A. Robinson, ed., *The Nag Hammadi Library in English,* 3rd ed. (San Francisco: Harper, 1990).

22. New York: Random House, 1979.

23. *Lost Christianities: The Battles for Scripture and the Faiths We Never Knew* (New York: Oxford University Press, 2003).

24. Ehrman, *Lost Christianities,* 255.

Galatians 1:8-9; 2 Corinthians 10–13; Jude). Daniel L. Hoffman has painstakingly refuted the central theses of Elaine Pagels.[25] Simon Gathercole's learned study demonstrates that, far from a narrow orthodox unity being extracted from a rich diversity, the flow went the other way: first to develop was the strong confessionalism; and then, as the passage of time and the pressures from the surrounding cultures spawned more and more aberrant theologies, Christians were forced to devote more thought to formulations that excluded these new aberrations precisely because they had never been part of the Christian heritage.[26] A recent book by Charles Hill demonstrates that the fourfold Gospel structure that we know in the New Testament was *not* invented in the fourth century but was already well known in the second, by thinkers as diverse as Hippolytus, Tertullian, Origen, Dionysius, Cyprian, Victorinus, Marinus, Euplus, and, of course, Irenaeus.[27] It does not seem unreasonable to infer that the devotion to diversity that marks so much of contemporary culture lies behind not a little of the revisionist historiography.[28]

Truth Addressing Sin and Redemption In popular thought, religions like Islam and Christianity are less tolerant because they say that others are wrong, whereas a religion like Buddhism is acceptable because it refuses to say that others are wrong. Doubtless there are Western "liberal" distortions of Buddhism that are endlessly open to other religious stances, just as there are liberal distortions of Christianity that talk about the "essence" of Christianity in similar terms. Yet Buddhism is not as open to other religions as many think. When the Dalai Lama was asked whether only the Buddha can provide "the ultimate source of refuge," he replied:

25. *The Status of Women and Gnosticism in Irenaeus and Tertullian,* Studies in Women and Religion 36 (Lewiston: Mellen, 1995).

26. Simon J. Gathercole, *"E pluribus unum?* Apostolic Unity and Early Christian Literature," in *"But My Words Will Never Pass Away": The Enduring Authority of the Christian Scriptures,* ed. D. A. Carson, 2 vols. (Grand Rapids: Eerdmans, forthcoming).

27. *Who Chose the Gospels? Probing the Great Gospel Conspiracy* (New York: Oxford University Press, 2010).

28. Cf. Andreas J. Köstenberger and Michael J. Kruger, *The Heresy of Orthodoxy: How Contemporary Culture's Fascination with Diversity Has Reshaped Our Understanding of Early Christianity* (Wheaton: Crossway, 2010).

Here, you see, it is necessary to examine what is meant by liberation or salvation. Liberation in which "a mind that understands the sphere of reality annihilates all defilements in the sphere of reality" is a state that only Buddhists can accomplish. This kind of *moksha* or *nirvana* is only explained in the Buddhist scriptures, and is achieved only through Buddhist practice.[29]

In other words, a religion may make exclusive claims even while acknowledging that other religions say important things.[30]

What we must learn from this observation, I think, are two things. *First,* the fundamental issues that divide religions are more than discrete propositions (though certainly not less). For example, at the propositional level, Christians believe Jesus is the only human being to be worshiped as God, while Muslims say the notion of any human being worshiped as God is blasphemous, and the various sectors of Buddhism have such different notions of the divine that the Christian confession is not easily parsed in their categories. These three world religions — and of course we could have added others, such as Hinduism, to the discussion — differ in more than a handful of christological propositions. These propositions are intertwined with what we think of God, with what we think salvation consists in and how it is or is not achieved, with how one views the world, with how one diagnoses the deepest human problems, with one's relationship with God (or with some notion of the divine). In short, these three religions embrace amazingly diverse views of what salvation consists in, of what the divine is like, of how one is "saved." In Christian terms, there are massive and coherent perceptions about the entire drama of sin and redemption — yet even to put it like that is to stipulate a decisively *Christian* way of looking at the world. These perceptions simply

29. His Holiness the XIVth Dalai Lama, "'Religious Harmony' and The Bodhgaya Interviews," in *Christianity through Non-Christian Eyes,* ed. Paul J. Griffiths (Maryknoll: Orbis, 1990), 169. I am indebted for the reference to Keith Yandell and Harold Netland, *Buddhism: A Christian Exploration and Appraisal* (Downers Grove: InterVarsity, 2009), 109.

30. On Buddhist views of other religions, see K. N. Jayatilleke, *The Buddhist Attitude to Other Religions* (Kandy: Buddhist Publication Society, 1975); Kristin Beise Kiblinger, *Buddhist Inclusivism: Attitudes towards Religious Others* (Burlington: Ashgate, 2005).

do not work together in any other religion — just as other religions have their own perceptions about the world and religious reality. It is simply unfair to *any* of them to pretend they are all saying the same thing.

One understands the pragmatic reasons why Miroslav Volf wants to convince us that Christians and Muslims worship the same God,[31] but it is hard to be convinced that he has it quite right. Historically, Islam is an offshoot of one branch of Christendom, so in that sense there is a genetic connection — but even this way of framing Muslim history would be disputed by Muslims themselves, who see Islam as a fresh prophetic word that corrects both Judaism and Christianity, not least the latter's trinitarianism. In any pair of monotheistic religions, one can always list the commonalities, for some commonalities are almost inevitable. But we must press farther. For example, at one point Volf argues that when Muslims love their neighbors, they are worshiping the one true God, and he quotes 1 John 4:7-8, 16b to prove it: "Dear friends, let us love one another, for love comes from God. Everyone who loves has been born of God and knows God. Whoever does not love does not know God, because God is love. . . . God is love. Whoever lives in love lives in God, and God in them."[32] Such love may say nothing about the eternal state of anyone, but it does tie all genuine love to God as its source. But what Volf leaves out at the ellipsis must not be overlooked: "This is how God showed his love among us: He sent his one and only Son into the world that we might live through him. This is love: not that we loved God, but that he loved us and sent his Son as an atoning sacrifice for our sins. Dear friends, since God so loved us, we also ought to love one another" (1 John 4:9-11). In other words, the Christian understanding of love is tied irretrievably to Jesus' death on the cross, by which he expiated sin and propitiated the Father's wrath (he is "an atoning sacrifice for our sins") — the very things that Muslims view as, at best, superstition, but that Christians see as lying at the very heart of who God is and what he has done, *and of how we are to understand what love is.* The entire fabric of Christian theology is tied to the grace of God by which he

---

31. *Allah: A Christian Response* (New York: HarperOne, 2011).
32. Volf, *Allah: A Christian Response,* 120.

saves his people through the cross and resurrection of his Son; the entire fabric of Muslim thought (most Muslims prefer not to think of it as "theology") is tied to earning your way to acceptance by Allah the Merciful.[33] These are not minor divergences.

Again, when Jesus is asked, "Show us the Father" (John 14:8), he replies, "Don't you know me, Philip, even after I have been among you such a long time? Anyone who has seen me has seen the Father. How can you say, 'Show us the Father'?" (14:9). It appears, then, at this point in redemptive history, that *not* to recognize who Jesus is, is *not* to know God.

Volf wants to minimize the differences between Christians and Muslims not least because, having emerged from the deadly violence of the Balkans, he hopes that such an agenda will lessen the antipathy between the groups and therefore reduce the threat of violence. The goal is wholly admirable, but it is a profoundly intellectualist approach to conflict reduction. It is far from clear how much of the bloodshed in the Balkans was rooted in religion, and how much in politics, tribalism, conflict over land, feuds grounded in competing histories, a culture of the vendetta, and so on. Meanwhile, insofar as this or any other Christian/Muslim conflict *is* religious, the issue is never *merely* religious/theological, but is also bound up with how each side views the place of *coercion.*

In the third chapter of this book I deal with some of the Christian history of the tension between tolerance (in the old sense) and coercion. I shall return in the seventh chapter to the shape of this tension in a democratic society. But it is worth reminding ourselves that Muslim thought runs along lines quite different to Christian wrestlings over the relationship between church and state. Where Muslims are in control, Muslim thought about non-Muslims in the society is quite clear. The choices are three: kill them (under certain circumstances), convert them, or *dhimmitude.*[34] The *dhimmis* (i.e., the non-Muslims in the culture) are inevitably placed in an inferior position. They may pay more taxes; they may not attempt to convert Mus-

33. A Muslim scholar like Shabbir Akhtar (cited in note 16 above) does not *concede* these points; rather, he *insists* on them.

34. See the important book by Mark Durie and Bat Ye'or, *The Third Choice: Islam, Dhimmitude and Freedom* (Melbourne: Deror Books, 2010).

lims to their own faith; any compromise they propose to stabilize their position will inevitably be taken as a mark of their inferiority and weakness, for, from a devout Muslim perspective, the *dhimmis* frankly owe homage to Allah and his people. Stances that the West perceives to be gracious, offered in the name of compromise, are likely to be taken as what is owed. Volf's book, I fear, will play well with many Westerners, while it will be read by many devout Muslims as evidence of the moral compromise and increasing weakness of Christians. In other words, Volf is not arguing that peace is more likely if each side argues its position forcefully but with respect and courtesy, but that peace is more likely if we emphasize lowest-common-denominator theology. That fits very well into the current climate in the West; in Muslim thought, it is a mark of the impending *dhimmitude* of Western peoples.[35]

The point of these reflections is simply to show that more than isolated propositions are disputed between major religions. There are entire matrices of beliefs, amounting to competing worldviews about what I have called "sin and redemption."

The *second* thing to learn is that the secular frame of reference that grounds so much of the new tolerance is, from one perspective, no less religious than the religions it seeks to displace. If the secularist protests that this is a ridiculous claim because he or she does not believe in God — at least, not the sort of God who makes large demands on our lives and on the lives of others — we reply, "Neither do many Buddhists." If the secularist protests, "But my way really is superior, for it is most grounded in the truth of reality itself," then recall that the Dalai Lama says much the same thing about Buddhism. The chief difference is that *while the secularist wants all other religions to retreat into the private sphere, he or she insists that secularists have the right to control the public sphere because they are right — completely unaware that they are trying to impose their worldview on others who disagree with it.* Others, they say, are intolerant because they say those with whom they disagree are wrong. But of course the secularists are

---

35. Cf. Shabbir Akhtar, *Islam as Political Religion*, 37-38: "A permanent stalemate persists between a prophetic monotheism which must arrest the divine engagement at the level of prophetic instruction and an incarnational theology which sees gracious possibilities beyond messengers bringing laws and divine punishment."

no less insistent that those who disagree with them are wrong, yet never entertain a guilty wisp of thought suggesting that perhaps they themselves are intolerant.

In short, this truth question catches up with *all* of us. And it affects our broadest visions of what we think is wrong with the world, and how to address it. All of us think in terms of (our own equivalents of) sin and redemption.

Truth and Love   It is not uncommon for the new tolerance to pit truth against love in a zero-sum game: one or the other will be diminished. If your church has a statement of faith, you may be trying to uphold truth, but love for outsiders will be diminished. If you think of Christian faith as bound up with articulating, proclaiming, and defending the truth, you will diminish in love, for truth draws borders and establishes that those who disagree with you are "other," and the inevitable result is lovelessness and intolerance. You cannot truly love and be passionate for truth.

Biblically speaking, this is a strange position, however popular it is today. For instance, in his first letter the apostle John establishes three tests of genuine Christian profession: a truth test (believers must believe certain things to be true), a love test (believers must genuinely love one another), and an obedience test (believers must do what Jesus says). Transparently, all of us fail these tests, more or less frequently — and then the only comfort John provides (and it is entirely sufficient) is that the blood of Jesus, God's Son, cleanses us from all sin. The point to observe is that these three tests must be applied *together:* it is not best two out of three, nor is there an option to excel in one and flunk the other two. In particular, John senses no discomfort in pushing *both* truth *and* love. One must conclude, therefore, that if we are tempted to pit one against the other, then clearly there is something fundamentally amiss in our conception of truth, of love, or of both.

In the words of the always quotable C. S. Lewis:

> Love is something more stern and splendid than mere kindness: . . . even the love between the sexes is, as in Dante, "a lord of terrible aspect." There is kindness in Love: but Love and kindness are not coterminous, and when kindness (in the sense given above) is

separated from the other elements of Love, it involves a certain fundamental indifference to its object, and even something like contempt of it. Kindness consents very readily to the removal of its object — we have all met people whose kindness to animals is constantly leading them to kill animals lest they should suffer. Kindness, merely as such, cares not whether its object becomes good or bad, provided only that it escapes suffering. As Scripture points out, it is bastards who are spoiled: the legitimate sons, who are to carry on the family tradition, are punished [Heb. 12:8]. It is for people whom we care nothing about that we demand happiness on any terms: with our friends, our lovers, our children, we are exacting and would rather see them suffer much than be happy in contemptible and estranging modes. If God is Love, He is, by definition, something more than mere kindness. And it appears, from all the records, that though He has often rebuked us and condemned us, He has never regarded us with contempt. He has paid us the intolerable compliment of loving us, in the deepest, most tragic, most inexorable sense.[36]

Truth and Evangelism   As soon as we see that the category of "truth" is a non-negotiable element of any religion that is taken seriously, what Christians think of as evangelism and what many in our culture condemn as proselytism take on a rather different flavor. Proselytism is largely despised, partly because one of the residues of postmodernism is a reluctance to tell others they are mistaken (at least in some domains), and partly because religion itself is seen to be a matter of private and highly subjective opinion, and therefore not the sort of thing one should be trying to foist on others. But if, say, Christianity insists that at its heart lies good news about what God has done in Christ Jesus, news about God that is true, news about what God has done in Christ Jesus that is true, news that alone can save people from the wrath to come, then Christians *ought* to talk about it and seek to win others to it. It would be unconscionable *not* to do so, not only because it is the truth but because it is truth of unimaginably great importance.

To list such efforts as marks of intolerance is, at best, an in-

36. C. S. Lewis, *The Problem of Pain* (New York: HarperOne, 2001), 32-33.

stance of the pot calling the kettle black. Those who make such pronouncements are trying to convince others of *their* perspective, in an ongoing debate in which *their* perspective, which they regard as the truth, is not accepted to be true by countless millions of people. Much better, then, to let the competing parties try to persuade others of the truthfulness of their views, *without the manipulative bludgeoning of the other party by labeling it intolerant.*

Truth and Tolerance: Concluding Reflections

(1) Religion without truth. A remarkable recent book is about and by three women: a Muslim, a Christian, and a Jew.[37] Ranya Idliby is a Muslim; Suzanne Oliver was a Catholic and is now an Episcopalian; Priscilla Warner is a Jew. Initially they started meeting together in 2002 to produce a children's book centered on common ties and stories shared by Jews, Christians, and Muslims, all of whom link back to the shared figure of Abraham. They acknowledge that wariness and suspicion characterized their early meetings, but they became fast friends. Not only did they finish their children's book, but they wrote *The Faith Club,* which relates their journey. Today when they meet in Oliver's apartment, sharing their jokes, finishing one another's sentences, and downing snacks, their honesty, candor, and perseverance have transparently paid off in genuine friendship.

The interesting thing is that the women themselves say that those who read, say, the Qur'an or the Bible literally, rather than metaphorically or with generous allowance made for cultural context, will find the views of the three women too liberal. In other words, if someone takes the teaching of their respective authoritative books seriously, holding that there is precisely one way to God and to heaven, recognizing that there are competing truth claims that cannot responsibly be swept aside in the warmth of good coffee, the model of *The Faith Club* may seem less satisfactory.[38]

37. Ranya Idliby, Suzanne Oliver, and Priscilla Warner, *The Faith Club: A Muslim, a Christian, a Jew* (New York: Free Press, 2007).

38. *The Faith Club* is of course not the only example of contentless agreement. Also in 2007, Rev. Ann Homes Redding, an Episcopal Church priest in Seattle, declared

To put the matter another way, interfaith dialog, whether in formal settings or in coffee klatches, will likely come to this sort of happy friendship *provided no participant believes very much to be true within his or her respective traditions.* A Muslim who believes very little and a Christian who believes very little and a Jew who believes very little will have a lot in common: very little. No wonder they are in agreement. They do not disagree over very much, and therefore happily agree. Really interesting dialog would take place, however, if believers showed up who happily articulate the exclusive claims of their respective religions. Then one would discover whether or not genuine tolerance (in the first sense) will prevail: honest debate where each side can feel free to say others are wrong, without fear of coercion by the state. Such friendship, when it occurs, is truly valuable; the friendship of *The Faith Club* is largely narcissistic.

(2) "Tolerance" without convictions. G. K. Chesterton is reputed to have said, "Tolerance is the virtue of a man without convictions." That is true under the second definition of tolerance. Under the first understanding of tolerance, however memorable the line, it is not quite true. Under the first definition, tolerance is the virtue of a person with convictions who thinks that others should not be coerced to agree with his convictions. B. B. Warfield understood the distinction more than a century ago. In 1887 Phillips Brooks, the Rector of Trinity Church, Boston, published two lectures on tolerance. War-

---

herself both a Christian and a Muslim. Responding to questions about her beliefs, she replied, "I believe that Jesus is divine in the same way in which all humans are related to God as children of God. Jesus is different in degree, not kind; that means that he shows me most fully what it means to be in total submission to and identification with God. The significance of his crucifixion is that it is the ultimate surrender, and the resurrection — both his and as it is revealed in the lives of his disciples — shows us that God makes life out of death. That is the good news to me and it is salvation. I don't think God said, 'Let me send this special person so that I can kill him for the benefit of the rest of humanity.' That's not the kind of sacrifice I think that God desires." In other words, she denies central teachings of confessional Christianity. Yet she also affirms that Jesus died and rose again, which denies what the Qur'an teaches. Her bishop, the Right Reverend Vincent Warner, declares that Rev. Redding's claim that she is both a Christian and a Muslim is exciting in terms of interfaith understanding. In fact, it is incoherent. Or, as R. Albert Mohler puts it, "Is there any hope for a church whose bishop considers heresy to be exciting?" Cf. www.albertmohler.com/blog_read.php?id=964.

field approved of some of what Brooks wrote on the subject, but he also commented:

> [T]he kind of tolerance which Dr. Brooks most admires, "the tolerance which grows up in any man who is aware that truth is larger than his conception of it, and that what seems to be other men's errors must often be other parts of the truth of which he has only a portion," appears to us no tolerance at all, but catholicity of spirit. We are not "tolerant" of known or suspected truth; true tolerance comes into play only when we are confronted with what we recognize as error; and this is the reason why, as Dr. Brooks admirably argues, there can be no real tolerance in a mind which has no strong convictions and no firm grasp on truth.[39]

(3) Tolerance without religious liberty. Tolerance — whether the old kind or the new — is a different and less profound notion than the right to religious liberty. Governments may not support religious liberty and yet may choose for strategic or other reasons to be tolerant of certain religious beliefs and practices. By contrast, the concept of the *right* to religious liberty presupposes a particular understanding of human beings, of God, and of liberty. One dare not forget that the most cruelly oppressive regimes of the twentieth century were not led by Christian believers or by Muslim fundamentalists, but by Marxist atheists and Nazi theorists who uncompromisingly embraced secular creeds. They presupposed particular understandings of human beings, and therefore butchered millions of them; they presupposed particular understandings of God, and therefore denied his existence or conscripted him for their party's ends (Christians call that "idolatry"); they presupposed particular understandings of liberty, and therefore crushed it.

(4) Truth without the cross. One of the things that supporters of the new tolerance fear is the claim to truth that could easily turn totalitarian. But one of the remarkable features of Christianity is that at the heart of our faith is the Lord Jesus, who claims to *be* the truth

---

39. B. B. Warfield, "Reviews of Recent Theological Literature," *Presbyterian Review* 9, no. 33 (1888): 160. I am grateful to Fred Zaspel for drawing my attention to this passage.

(John 14:6) and yet who goes to the cross to save others. The exclusiveness of his claim is never diminished, yet this truth incarnate goes to the cross for the sake of others. While we insist on the power and non-negotiability of truth, we are also humbled by a God who in the person of his Son discloses truth crucified.

SIX

And Still There Is Evil

—◦◦◦—

In this short chapter, the focus is quite narrow. My aim is to show how reflecting on a variety of moral issues shines a little more light on the issues of tolerance and intolerance.

Morality and Truth

I have repeatedly argued that the new tolerance is nestled into some vision of truth largely shared by the culture or at least by the cultural elites. The issue then becomes what breaches of that vision can be tolerated, and whether social or even state coercion should ever be imposed when that vision of truth is violated, and if so, under what circumstances. Something similar could be said for the domain of moral conduct: in the older way of looking at things, certain conduct was approved and other conduct was frowned upon (invariably based on a complex mix of tradition, revelation, the state's instinct for its own preservation, cultural consensus, and the like). Questions of tolerance and intolerance were tied to the extent to which departure from such cultural norms might or might not be acceptable. Transparently, issues of truth and issues of morality were tied together. For example, it was morally wrong for, say, two men to sleep together, or for a man and a woman to commit adultery, because God had given the truth about how his image-bearers *ought* to behave. By contrast, the new tolerance has been largely cut free both from a well-articulated vision of truth and from binding culture-wide moral standards, and thus pretends to be the ultimate arbiter in both of these realms.

I have tried to show that these pretensions are sadly hollow. Because most of my attention in the previous chapter fastened on questions of truth, however, I paid only glancing attention to questions of morality. The supporters of the new tolerance, as we have seen, commonly think that they are advancing a higher morality. We must see clearly that this is not so.

The evidence surfaces in many forms. Consider, for instance, the increasing reluctance of many people under the influence of the new tolerance to take seriously the word "evil." One recalls the exchange between Dennis Miller and his fellow comedian Kathleen Madigan. It took place on Miller's CNBC television show on 7 September 2004. The discussion concerned the terrorists who killed more than two hundred people at a Russian school just a short while earlier. Miller asserted that it was right to label this act "evil"; Madigan disagreed. The discussion developed, in part, as follows:

> MILLER: Isn't it true, Kathleen, that Liberals, when they say the word 'evil' feel creeped out, because they tend to intellectualize it and . . . they don't want to thump the Bible, so they won't say evil. But when you shoot a kid 45 times . . . is there a place on the face of this planet holier than a grade school on the first day of school? We've got to go to the mat with these people.
>
> MADIGAN: Evil. It's just a word. Like, for me it just brings up Catholic grade school, nothing good comes up in my head. I say wacked, how about wacked?
>
> MILLER: No, evil. This is one time I can't join the joke. We have to concede that these people . . . [interrupted]
>
> MADIGAN: I'm serious! I just think that word has a connotation that brings too much religion to it in my head. Yeah, these are bad people, it's awful, but when [President Bush] gets up there and goes 'they're evil and we're the good guys' . . . I think it definitely brings this whole religion thing into it that he's got going on in his head.
>
> GUEST: So what?

MADIGAN: So, that's not what's going on in my head, so I don't agree with it.

The editor of the piece where this exchange is reported comments, "A few decades ago the word 'sin' became scarce in all but religious circles (with the one exception of the dessert menu). Perhaps the word evil is heading in the same direction."[1]

A little over thirty years ago, the media could use the word "evil" without embarrassment. In a moving essay in *Time,* devoted to reflecting on the horrific slaughter in Cambodia perpetrated by Pol Pot and his collaborators, David Aikman wrote:

> In the West today, there is a pervasive consent to the notion of moral relativism, a reluctance to admit that absolute evil can and does exist. This makes it especially difficult for some to accept the fact that the Cambodian experience is something far worse than a revolutionary aberration. Rather, it is the deadly logical consequence of an atheistic, man-centered system of values, enforced by fallible human beings with total power, who believe, with Marx, that morality is whatever the powerful define it to be and, with Mao, that power grows from gun barrels. By no coincidence the most humane Marxist societies in Europe today are those that, like Poland or Hungary, permit the dilution of their doctrine by what Solzhenitsyn has called "the great reserves of mercy and sacrifice" from a Christian tradition.[2]

Of course, if we cannot bring ourselves to classify the most horrendous genocide as evil, we are unlikely to think through ways in which all human beings are evil, ways in which the germ of the moral darkness lies within all of us. When James Waller published his book, arguing that evidence shows that the Nazi Holocaust was carried out by ordinary people and not a nation of sociopaths,[3] reviewers went to

---

1. See the report in *Modern Reformation* 13, no. 6 (2004).

2. *Time,* 31 July 1978; now available at http://www.time.com/time/magazine/article/0,2171,946921-3,00.html. Much of the same passage is also cited in Don Cormack, *Killing Fields, Living Fields* (London: Monarch, 1997), 176.

3. James Waller, *Becoming Evil: How Ordinary People Commit Genocide and Mass Killing* (Oxford: Oxford University Press, 2002).

extraordinary lengths to show that the thesis simply had to be wrong.[4] For obviously if the thesis is right, ordinary people can easily become sociopaths. Frankly, Waller more closely reflects biblical insight than do his critics. For although the Bible delights in "common grace" — the grace that God graciously distributes commonly to people — it is ruthlessly realistic about what lies in the human heart (e.g., Romans 3:9-20).

Once the category of evil disappears, our moral discernment has no structure. Strong fiber is reduced to mush; the skeleton of moral reasoning is taken out, and what is left is jelly-like protoplasm. We end up not only with rampant ethical relativism but with the anemic inability to feel or express moral outrage over pervasive immorality.[5] The failure to recognize the evil in our own hearts is precisely what convinces so many of us that our opinions and motives are above reproach while those who contradict us are stupid or malign. A healthy dose of Augustinian realism about sin, as Mark Ellingsen puts it, could make America a better place: indeed, that is why the founding fathers cared so much about checks and balances, about constitutional limitations, about division of powers: they did not trust anyone precisely because the founders had a robust notion of sin.[6] If in our environment the virtue of (the new) tolerance becomes absolute, then ostensibly moral discussions are brought round to this one consideration. For example, in a recent report by the Australia Institute titled "Mapping Homophobia in Australia," we are told that 62 percent of evangelical Christians are homophobic. The evidence? People were asked whether they agreed or disagreed with the statement, "I believe that homosexuality is immoral." If they agreed, they were classified as homophobic.[7] In other words, there was no moral engagement with the complexities surrounding human sexuality, but merely a label used to brand an entire class of people with the supreme shame: in-

---

4. E.g., Alan Wolfe, "Desperately Wicked: Reckoning with Evil," *Books & Culture* 9, no. 2 (March/April 2003): 26-27.

5. Cf. Harry Blamires, *The Post-Christian Mind: Exposing Its Destructive Agenda* (Ann Arbor: Servant, 1999).

6. Mark Ellingsen, *Blessed Are the Cynical: How Original Sin Can Make America a Better Place* (Grand Rapids: Brazos, 2002).

7. Reported in *The Briefing* 328 (January 2006).

tolerance. Again: Millions call themselves "pro-choice" in the matter of abortion. But that is coherent for them because abortion itself is morally neutral, and therefore the choice is devoid of moral significance except for its availability to the sovereign freedom of the individual will.[8] Small wonder that we have arrived at the place where our medical experts can help generate life in the womb, and can kill a baby about to emerge from the womb, with no moral differentiation. It is merely a matter of personal choice.

Clearly, we must hone in for a while on:

Morality and Relativism

One of the finest brief statements of relativism of which I am aware is the address by John Piper, "The Challenge of Relativism," delivered at the Ligonier Conference in 2007, and subsequently developed and published.[9] With his permission, I reproduce or adapt some of his points here, before turning the discussion to our own concerns.

Piper begins by asking, "How is the bad thing called relativism different from good ways of thinking relatively?" We may conclude that someone is tall or short relative to another person: in many domains, such thinking is not only a useful way of thinking but an indispensable way of thinking. When we make such comparisons, people on all sides have some kind of measurement standard in their minds, so the relative height or shortness of two people is agreed on the basis of a shared standard.

But relativ*ism* is different. For moral relativism to exist, one or more of the following statements must be true:

(1) There is no external or objective standard of truth.
(2) The standard *may* be out there, but we cannot know it.
(3) The standard *is* out there, but we cannot know what it means.

8. This example is helpfully discussed in the acerbically unfashionable book by David Bentley Hart, *Atheist Delusions: The Christian Revolution and Its Fashionable Enemies* (New Haven: Yale University Press, 2009).

9. John Piper, *Think: The Life of the Mind and the Love of God* (Wheaton: Crossway, 2010), chaps. 7-8 (pp. 89-112).

(4) The standard exists and we can know what it means, but we simply do not care.

Consider the statement, "Sexual relations between two human males is wrong." Two people might disagree over the truthfulness of this statement and still not be relativists. For instance, they might both hold that the Bible is God's authoritative Word and that it establishes an external, objective standard on this matter, but might disagree as to what the Bible says. Relativism arises when there is no standard, or when the standard is said to exist but we cannot know what it means (or any of the four points listed above). Perhaps the saddest (and certainly the ugliest) relativism is found under the fourth point. It is a kind of pragmatic relativism: we acknowledge the standards but insist on doing things our own way — in much the same way that we can have a pragmatic atheism (we know that God exists but we act as if he doesn't).

Relativism is the view that no one standard of true and false, right and wrong, good and bad, beautiful and ugly exists that is valid for everyone. Relativists may be happy to talk about my truth and your truth, but rarely about the truth. Convictions and conduct flow not from some objective standard but from personal or communal standards. Piper argues that pragmatic relativists exist in every culture: consider Matthew 21:21-27, where Jesus' opponents will not face the truth and so find ways to duck it, even to say untrue things in order to preserve their own lies. The tragic reality of our generation in the West (though certainly not everywhere in the world) is that we have codified and authorized relativism to such a degree that interest in truth and morality alike, in any enduring and objective sense, has largely dissolved.

From the perspective of the Bible, relativism is treason against God and his Word. That the God of the Bible exists establishes the possibility of truth; that he is a revealing God establishes the possibility of knowing that truth. Relativism regularly plays games with language, encourages doctrinal aberration, cultivates duplicity, and pretends to be humble while authorizing astonishing arrogance. Relativism promises freedom but enslaves people: it refuses to acknowledge sin and evil the way the Bible does, and therefore it never adequately confronts sin and evil, and therefore leaves people enslaved by sin and evil. Even at societal levels, it is an invitation to destruction, for if everyone does that which is right in their own eyes, the end is either anarchic chaos or cultural cries for more laws in order to establish stability — ultimately even a call for a dictator.

When we witness the new tolerance making its way through this miasma, we understand, once again, through this new optic, how controlling discussions of tolerance and intolerance can be, *precisely because there are no other widely agreed categories for right and wrong.* And for exactly the same reason, such discussion cannot be leavened by networks of broader moral considerations: there aren't any, or at least not many.[10]

Morality and Tolerance

The effect of this change is striking. It used to be that the moral issues held a central place in public discourse, and part of that discourse dealt with how much deviation from those moral standards could be tolerated. Increasingly, however, the rights and wrongs of the old moral issues receive scant attention while the public discourse focuses on what sanctions should be imposed on those who do not "tolerate" (definitely the new sense!) the abolition of what were once the

---

10. This problem surfaces in many disciplines, yet among those most committed to unqualified open-endedness, the seriousness of the problem is rarely confronted. One thinks, for instance, of the book by Susan E. Gillingham, *One Bible, Many Voices* (Grand Rapids: Eerdmans, 1998). She argues at length that both the diversity of content in the Bible and the diversity of approaches to its interpretation drive us to the conclusion that the Bible has "many voices," not one. In short, we must insist on a pluralistic approach to the Bible. But then in her conclusion (pp. 245-47), she recalls the warning of Anthony Thiselton (*New Horizons in Hermeneutics: The Theory and Practice of Transforming Bible Study* [New York: HarperCollins, 1992], 612), who carefully warns against the authoritarian pluralism that disguises itself as liberal pluralism. As soon as we insist that the only responsible way to read the Bible is in a thoroughly pluralistic fashion, we have narrowed our theory down to one dogmatic option — which is of course what Gillingham has done. She acknowledges the problem: "An appeal to read the Bible in a pluralistic way is thus in need of some sort of self-critique" (p. 245). Yet the most she can winkle out of this observation is that while we defend pluralism "we should be as critical of pluralism *per se* as we should be critical of any exclusivist approach" (p. 247). But if we are *that* critical of pluralistic approaches, might we not be driven to wondering if there are not some certainties grounded in Scripture?

moral standards. In other words, the primary "moral" line drawn through Western culture declares that those who "tolerate" just about anything are good, and those who do not are bad and therefore should not be tolerated.

The most striking test case is homosexuality. Not for a moment should anyone deny that the evidence as to what "makes" a homosexual is extraordinarily complex. Few have matched the care and objectivity of the study by Stanton L. Jones and Mark A. Yarhouse.[11] In popular discourse, however, virtually none of that complexity is allowed to surface in the public square. It is everywhere assumed that people are simply born that way, and that's all there is to it. Even if that were the case — and the evidence simply will not allow such shallow reductionism — it would not in itself establish that the practice of homosexuality is a good thing, absent a number of other assumptions.

My intention at the moment is not to document the way evidence is regularly presented in highly manipulative fashion (e.g., the media find one homosexual couple who have loved each other dearly for forty years, and contrast it with a scrappy heterosexual couple on their respective third marriages laced with physical abuse, without probing the abundant statistics of how infrequent homosexual fidelity is), but to observe how the media regularly blacken the character of anyone who entertains the possibility that homosexual behavior is not a good thing. One remembers, for instance, that when President George W. Bush proposed James Holsinger for the post of Surgeon General, someone discovered that twenty years earlier Holsinger had voted with the majority of the United Methodist Judicial Council to continue the ban on ordaining practicing homosexuals. The *Boston Globe* demanded that Bush withdraw the nomination of Holsinger, since "no one should go into the job with a record of discriminating against people because of their sexual orientation."[12] The *Washington*

11. Stanton L. Jones and Mark A. Yarhouse, *Homosexuality: The Use of Scientific Research in the Church's Moral Debate* (Downers Grove: InterVarsity, 2000). Cf. also Peter Sprigg and Timothy Dailey, eds., *Getting It Straight: What the Research Shows about Homosexuality* (Washington: Family Research Council, 2004).

12. 19 June 2007. The article can now be read at http://www.boston.com/news/globe/editorial_opinion/editorials/articles/2007/06/19/intolerance_makes_bad _medicine/.

Post was positively derisive.[13] At no point was the issue of homosexual practice itself seriously discussed. Rather, all the focus was on the "intolerance" of Holsinger, which in much editorial opinion was ground for banning him from high office. In the name of tolerance, his appointment was not to be tolerated.[14]

Similar intolerance is no less common in Europe. In the autumn of 2004, Rocco Buttiglione, Italy's representative to the European Union, was rejected as its commissioner for justice on the ground that he is a Catholic who agrees with his church's stance on homosexuality. At his hearings he carefully distinguished between what is immoral and what should be criminal, but of course the EU authorities could not allow any deviation from their secular agenda, for this would mean fostering intolerance.

Again, in 2010 Kenneth Howell found himself in difficulty with the University of Illinois at Champaign-Urbana. At the time, Howell was both Director of the Newman Center's Institute of Catholic Thought and adjunct professor in the University. He was teaching a course titled "Introduction to Catholicism and Modern Catholic Thought." In response to discussion in the classroom regarding homosexuality, on 4 May he distributed a three-page email to his students clarifying some points of Catholic thought on the subject, dealing with natural law theory, and with the subject line "Utilitarianism and Sexuality." A month later, a student who was not taking the class, but who had seen the email sent to one of his friends who *was* taking the class, complained to Howell's department head in the University, arguing, among other things, "Teaching a student about the tenets of religion is one thing. Declaring that homosexual acts violate the natu-

13. 14 June 2007, available now at http://www.washingtonpost.com/wp-dyn/content/article/2007/06/13/AR2007061302012.html.

14. Many more examples of this sort could be adduced. For example, in 2003, when William H. Pryor Jr., then Attorney General of Arkansas, was nominated to the U.S. Court of Appeals for the Eleventh Circuit, Senator Charles Schumer, Democrat of New York, objected on the ground that Pryor's beliefs were so well known and so deeply held that it was hard to believe they would not influence his decisions. In other words, we may not bar a person from high office on the ground of race or creed, provided the creed is so loosely held that it exercises no influence on his conduct. In a word, the necessary positive criterion is the adoption of a tacit secularism.

ral laws of man is another."[15] The argument is itself very revealing: *religion has no right to deal with moral questions* — and meanwhile, the *real* offense is the suggestion that something is wrong when a lot of people think it is right.

The department head, Robert McKim, argued that the University has an interest in not making students feel uncomfortable, which of course brought the meaning of "intolerance" to a new level of plasticity. Before the brouhaha had ended, Howell, backed into a corner, defended his right to teach as he did on the ground of his First Amendment right to free speech. The University fired him, but sufficient uproar ensued that eventually the University hired him back. The reason why Howell prevailed, of course, was not because his moral arguments became convincing to the University authorities, but because both those who found Howell's email reasonable and those who found it despicable converged in protest against what they saw as the University's disregard for academic freedom: in short, the university was intolerant in its defense of tolerance. That was the only "moral" issue.

In short, whether one is seeking high political office or attempting to maintain an unpopular position in an academic environment — to say nothing of wanting to win a beauty queen pageant, as the experience of Carrie Prejean shows — enormous pressures are mounted to keep out, in the name of tolerance, those who hold, however courteously, that homosexual practice is wrong.

These are the milder instances of denunciation against those who question the unobjectionable nature of homosexual relations. The wilder examples — and there are many — are common and cruel.[16] In addition to the irony that these are often offered in defense

15. The matter has been very widely discussed. One of the most comprehensive reports is "Fired, in a Crowded Theater," *First Things* 2006 (October 2010): 24-29.

16. For example, in several Western countries street preachers have been arrested (and occasionally convicted) for saying that homosexuality is wrong, citing the Bible. In the UK, a couple has been banned from fostering children because they taught their foster children that homosexual practice is wrong. In several countries, it is no longer impossible to imagine how clergy may be prosecuted for refusing to offer civil union ceremonies, or even marriage ceremonies, under church aegis. More broadly, the media insist on referring to the horrible abuse of boys by priests as "pedophilia," even though it is not: pedophilia is the sexual molestation of very young

of (the new) tolerance, there is a sadder irony: genuine homophobia, with its own wanton cruelty, when it is lumped together with mere affirmations that homosexual practice is wrong, begins to get a free pass because the charges against the latter group are sooner or later seen as the empty and scurrilous hate-mongering they are. Perhaps no one has commented on this more trenchantly than the social critic Camille Paglia:

> For gays to demand that sincere Christians cease lobbying Washington about the increasing liberal drift of government policy shows colossal historical amnesia. For pity's sake, it was the flamboyant, thunderous activism of evangelical Protestant ministers in the 19th century that powered the abolitionist movement and led to the end of slavery in the United States. (Of course, these massively documented facts were concealed in Steven Spielberg's Liberal Hollywood Lite version of "Amistad.") . . .
>
> Similarly, eloquent Protestant ministers like Martin Luther King Jr. and Jesse Jackson have been central to the modern Civil Rights Movement, which secured voting rights for African-Americans and opened the way to the election of a rising number of black politicians at the local, state and federal levels. So gays should quit bitching about Southern Baptists exercising their constitutional right to free speech about homosexuality, which is indeed condemned by the Bible, despite the tortuous casuistry of so many self-interested parties, including clerics. I have been warning and warning for years that the insulting disrespect shown by gay activists to religion — which has been going on for 20 years virtually unchecked on TV talk shows, with their biased liberal hosts — would produce a backlash over time. . . .
>
> As a libertarian, I believe that government must stay out of our private lives. As an atheist, I believe that government has no business sanctifying the unions of some persons (heterosexuals) but not others (homosexuals), particularly when certain benefits

---

children, while the abuse in question involved older boys, often teenagers. But where do the media speak of gay priests molesting teenage boys? See the discussion in Bernard Goldberg, *Arrogance: Rescuing America from the Media Elite* (New York: Warner Books, 2003), especially 165-84.

(such as employer-sponsored spousal health-insurance) flow to one group only.

As a scholar, however, I am troubled by the provincialism and amorality of the gay male world, when compared to the vastness of philosophical perspective provided by orthodox religion — or even by ancient paganism, which honored nature. And as a lesbian, I'm sick and tired of the gay rights movement being damaged by the cowardly incapacity for self-examination of many gay men.[17]

These are not abstract issues. A culture that minimizes values such as honor, integrity, valor, self-sacrifice for the sake of other people, truth-telling, and courtesy, while maximizing sexual freedom so strongly that the issues themselves cannot be debated because everything has been decided under the controlling rubric of the new tolerance, is destined in the long haul to pay horrendous costs.[18]

And Still There Is Evil

Supporters of the new tolerance seem to think that if everyone were as tolerant as they are, the world would be a far better place. We might even end war.

In reality, the genuine gains achieved by the new tolerance are slender in comparison with the losses. It has been moderately successful at diminishing demeaning epithets — "wogs," "chinks," and expressions of the same order. Even there the price is a certain kind of totalitarian political correctness. More serious, however, is the way the new tolerance swamps penetrating discussion about truth and morality: tolerance is widely perceived to be more important and more enduring than either. The result is a greater tendency to believe lies and to come adrift in immorality. Even in the political arena, as many wags have pointed out, the motto printed on United States cur-

17. From her column in *Salon,* accessible at http://www.salon.com/col/pagl/1998/06/nc_23pagl.html (2000).
18. Cf. R. Albert Mohler, *Desire and Deceit: The Real Cost of the New Sexual Tolerance* (Colorado Springs: Multnomah, 2008).

rency needs to be rewritten: *E Pluribus Unum* ("From the many, one") has *de facto* become *E Pluribus Plurus* ("From the many, many"). Many a Christian church and many a Christian parachurch organization devotes more attention to promoting its diversity than to fostering godly unity, even though in the Bible the diversity is not so much commanded as presupposed, while the unity is a desirable goal. Meanwhile, cultures in other parts of the world often see in Western (new) tolerance, not a mature and civilized culture worth emulating, but a childish and manipulative culture that refuses to engage with serious moral issues, and that is a danger to their own worlds owing to the power and reach of digital production.

Far from bringing peace, the new tolerance is progressively becoming more intolerant, fostering moral myopia, proving unable to engage in serious and competent discussions about truth, letting personal and social evils fester, and remaining blind to the political and international perceptions of our tolerant cultural profile.

SEVEN

Tolerance, Democracy, and Majoritarianism

—⌁∂∕∂⌁—

Although much of the contemporary public discourse regarding tolerance and intolerance revolves around individual rights, such rights derive from *somewhere:* from the state? from natural law? from the Creator? If from the state, do they really derive from the people if the government of that state is democratic? If there are limitations on tolerance — and, as we have seen, there always are — will such limitations be imposed by social sanction? by legal restrictions and the opinions of the courts? In other words, we cannot probe much farther into the challenges coughed up by tolerance, and especially the new tolerance, without a meditation on the state — especially, in the context where this book is written, democratic states.

Understanding the Problem

Robert P. George, McCormick Professor of Jurisprudence at Princeton University, tells of a meeting he attended of the American Constitution Society for Law and Policy. As he took his seat, he found on the desk in front of him a blue pamphlet that included the Declaration of Independence, Lincoln's Gettysburg Address, and the Constitution of the United States of America — thus a pocket-sized version of the nation's fundamental documents. He recalled having to memorize the Gettysburg Address when he was in the sixth grade, and to refresh his memory he read the Address again, including its final paragraph as reproduced in the pamphlet:

> It is rather for us to be here dedicated to the great task remaining before us — that, from these honored dead we take increased devotion to that cause for which they gave the last full measure of devotion — that we here highly resolve these dead shall not have died in vain — that this nation shall have a new birth of freedom, and that government of the people, by the people, and for the people, shall not perish from the earth.[1]

As anyone who has memorized the Gettysburg Address will note, the version published by the American Constitution Society for Law and Policy had left out words written and included by Lincoln: "that this nation, *under God,* shall have a new birth of freedom."

Inevitably there are academic disputes about which version is original, all of which George handles with his usual competence. It is hard to avoid the conclusion that powerful figures and institutions are willing to rewrite our history and even our foundation documents in order to achieve the secular order for which they long.

It is easy to duplicate stories like this. One particularly egregious instance of the abuse of court powers took place in the case of *Americans United for the Separation of Church and State v. Prison Fellowship Ministries* (2006). The case had to do with InnerChange Freedom Initiative (IFI), one of Prison Fellowship's programs to reduce recidivism. IFI is under contract with several state prison systems, working with prisoners before they are released, utilizing spiritual counseling, Bible study, and prayer. In Iowa, the AUSCS sued on the ground that for IFI to have a contract with the state (about 40 percent of their funding was from the state) constitutes an establishment of religion — indeed, a particularly sinister religion called evangelicalism. The evidence shows that IFI was remarkably effective in reducing recidivism, enhancing public safety, and reducing corrections costs, and no one disputed that evidence. Granted the way the establishment clause is commonly understood today (though more on this later), it is not sur-

---

1. Robert P. George, "God and Gettysburg," *First Things* 205 (August/September 2010): 15-17, esp. 16.

prising that Federal Judge Robert Pratt ruled against Prison Fellowship and ordered the Fellowship to reimburse the state to the tune of $1.5 million. What was shocking was that about thirty-five pages of the forty-page opinion found Judge Pratt justifying his ruling on *theological* grounds. Evangelicalism is "quite distinct from other self-described Christian faiths, such as Roman Catholicism, Mormonism, and Greek Orthodoxy. . . . [It] is also distinct from the beliefs held by self-described Protestant Christian denominations such as Lutheran, United Methodist, Episcopalian, and Presbyterian, to name only a few." Although Prison Fellowship's Statement of Faith "contains beliefs common to many types of Christian groups . . . it is also significantly different in many respects." For example, Judge Pratt complains, "The evangelical Christian stance towards religious institutions is one of suspicion." For example, they are "contemptuous of Roman Catholic reliance on papal authority, Marian devotion, and veneration of the saints." More shocking yet, "The Prison Fellowship and InnerChange believe in the substitutionary and atoning death of Jesus, which reflects a legalistic understanding of the sacrifice of Jesus and is likewise not shared by many Christians." Worse yet, they believe in the "literal, bodily resurrection of Christ." In fact, "A key concept in Chuck Colson's writings is that people must be born again."

This opinion is so laughably bad one wonders if space should be taken to refute it. Perhaps a few observations will not hurt. (1) Few other than Mormons themselves think of Mormonism as lying within the great tradition. (2) Evangelicalism is not some sect separate from, say, Methodism or Presbyterianism, since many in those traditions espouse it. (3) If evangelicalism is as contrary toward other faiths as Judge Pratt opines, and thus unable to work with denominations and other Christian groups, why is it so deeply embedded in huge swaths of, say, the Southern Baptist Convention, or the Presbyterian Church of America, or in organizations like Focus on the Family? Evangelicals disagree with Catholics on, say, Marian devotion or the authority of the pope, as Catholics disagree with evangelicals on the same issues. Does it follow that each is contemptuous of the other? Doesn't this sound as if Judge Pratt wants to rule out evangelicals on the ground that, in his view, they are not sufficiently *tolerant?* (4) Meanwhile, some of the items on Judge Pratt's list of distinctive evangelical doctrines, such as the substitutionary death of Christ or his bodily resurrection, are foundational to *every* confessional stream of Christianity; they are objected to primarily by those of such liberal persuasion that they want to weed out supernatural elements. (5) So Chuck Colson insists that people must be born again. But then again, so did Jesus (John 3). Does Judge Pratt want to blacklist some of Jesus' teachings by insisting that those who take Jesus seriously are sectarian? (6) But above all, what on earth does a federal judge think he is doing when he is blacklisting certain theological beliefs (the "sectarian" ones, as he understands the word) and not others? It is not his theological ignorance that is shocking, but his attempt to adjudicate such matters *in the name of keeping separate church and state.* His decision does not ban IFI on the ground that it is religious, but on the ground that it espouses forms of religion he personally does not like — and he thinks he has the theological insight to decide which forms of religious belief are acceptable. Where does the First Amendment give that sort of insight and discriminating power to the judiciary?

Mercifully, most of Judge Pratt's ruling was overturned about a year and a half later by the Eighth Circuit Court of Appeals, whose ruling made it a little clearer when faith-based organizations may legitimately work with governmental agencies.

Although it would be easy to provide a long list of such anecdotes, the real problem for our purposes might still be overlooked. Joseph Bottum crystallizes the issues rather nicely:

> It's a nudge here and a shove there. A push from one side and a kick from another. Little things, for the most part, and surprisingly often the perpetrators retreat when directly challenged, but only to watch someone else step in to take their place. . . .
>
> So the California court penalizes doctors for referring a patient to another clinic because they didn't want to perform in-vitro fertilization for an unmarried couple. A state representative in Connecticut submits legislation that would force the Catholic Church to divest itself of its parishes. A judge in Montana decides that healthcare providers are required to arrange for euthanasia when a patient requests it. The Equal Employment Opportunity Commis-

sion rules against a college in North Carolina for attempting not to provide its employees with health insurance that covers contraception. A charity in Massachusetts is forced out of the adoption business. The Ninth Circuit attempts to compel a park to remove a memorial cross rather than trade the land with the cross into private hands. A New Hampshire divorce court orders a Christian mother to stop homeschooling because her daughter "appeared to reflect her mother's rigidity on questions of faith." The president allows a diminished form of funding for faith-based institutions to continue, but only if these religious organizations stop hiring on the basis of their religion. An Illinois druggist is ordered to dispense abortifacients or to close his business. The blizzard of lawsuits to ban Christmas displays is beginning to fall on us once again, the most bizarre of the nation's holiday traditions.

Not one of these is a vital wound to the practice of American religion. Even together, they don't add up to anything like a death-blow.[2]

And yet, and yet. . . . As Bottum points out, the problem is not one particular episode, nor the aggregate of them, but their direction.

Small wonder that religious believers feel increasingly threatened and embattled. These kinds of mini-crises demonstrate that the route of purely privatized religion is not an option. Legislators, the courts, and the Executive Branch increasingly extend their reach by linking things together. You cannot be a pharmacist in some jurisdictions and *not* sell abortifacients; you cannot be an ob-gyn doctor in some jurisdictions and *not* perform abortions, even if you are willing to recommend another physician. You cannot say that something is wrong just because it offends anyone who can whisper in the ear of power. And in subtle ways, in the name of tolerance, state-sponsored *coercion* — the very criterion of what (the old) intolerance consists in — is brought to bear.

For democracies, like all governments, are based on affirming and supporting certain values and visions of reality, and proscribing others. But when the values and visions of reality that sustained such

2. Joseph Bottum, "A Demand for Freedom," *First Things* 198 (December 2009): 63.

democracies in the past shrivel away, in the domains where the shriveling takes place the only *über*-value is the new tolerance, backed up by the coercive power of the state. For example, when either capital punishment or euthanasia is discussed, proponents of various stances stake out their positions at least in part on the ground of the moral character of the proposed act. On some issues, however, such as abortion, even the disagreements over nomenclature reflect the confusion. Is third-term abortion by dilation and extraction "partial-birth abortion" or "murdering a viable infant"? Is abortion itself "terminating a fetus" or "murdering a baby"? As Scott Moore says,

> I believe that the move to redescription and trivialization is a consequence of our culture of convenience. Even before the pregnancy, sexuality itself has been redescribed and trivialized. It is not "consummation" but "hooking up." To separate the reproductive and the unitive dimensions of sexual intercourse radically transforms the nature of the act and the relationship within which it occurs.[3]

So the primary issue becomes the *rights* of the woman or the *rights* of the unborn infant, which in turn is tied to the extent to which the state *ought* to *tolerate* such-and-such conduct.

In classic liberal democracies, such discussions would signal a mad scramble to elect the appropriate legislators, for the legislators pass the laws, and the legislators alone are held accountable by the ballot box. In reality, in democracies with far-reaching and power-grabbing state and federal agencies, coupled with intrusive courts and international agencies, they signal a scramble to influence all the various branches of government. And, as we shall see, when the vision of what is "the good" becomes hugely polarized in any culture, such that widespread consensus is no longer possible, then it is not only a question of who "wins" or "loses" on any particular issue, but also a matter of the extent to which the opposing view is *tolerated*.

---

3. Scott H. Moore, *The Limits of Liberal Democracy: Politics and Religion at the End of Modernity* (Downers Grove: InterVarsity, 2009), 135.

Christianity, and Some Other Religious Faiths, Can Never Be Purely Private

Granted that at least a substantial part of the motivation that drove the pilgrim fathers to sail across the Atlantic into an unknown future was the passion for religious freedom, it is a betrayal of that heritage to argue for the privatization of religion. For privatized religion, as we have seen, is the only form of religion that the new tolerance is willing to tolerate.

Privatization of religion and religious freedom are not precisely inverse values, as if they belonged to some nefarious religious zero-sum game, yet some degree of inverse relationship exists. It may be helpful to spell this out.[4] Consider several worlds:

Option One: In this highly privatized world, citizens are permitted to think whatever they want about religious matters. How they practice their religion with others, however, may be monitored and highly controlled. There may be flowering rhetoric about freedom of religion — after all, people may believe whatever they like — but almost no genuine freedom when the religion becomes anything other than entirely private (e.g., passing on their beliefs to their children, worshiping with others in non-approved buildings, trying to win others to their faith).

Option Two: Citizens in this world have the right not only to hold on to whatever religious beliefs they like, but also to gather together with others who share similar beliefs. They are happy to be part of a religious community and tradition. From their point of view, this provides them with the freedom to explore the world from within this heritage; from the perspective of other citizens and of the state, they are harmless if somewhat eccentric. What they must *not* do, however, is actively proselytize (even if the believers themselves would prefer to think of such activity as evangelism, not proselytism). They themselves may of course convert to the dominant view of the culture, but

4. Helpful discussions are found in Stephen L. Carter, *The Dissent of the Governed: A Meditation on Law, Religion, and Loyalty* (Cambridge: Harvard University Press, 1998); and David Novak, *In Defense of Religious Liberty* (Wilmington: ISI Books, 2009); Barbara A. McGraw and Jo Renee Formicola, eds., *Taking Religious Pluralism Seriously: Spiritual Politics on America's Sacred Ground* (Waco: Baylor University Press, 2005).

those who hold to the dominant view must not under any circumstance convert to something other than the dominant view (which is the standard in many Muslim nations today).

Option Three: In this world, citizens may not only hold to their beliefs and meet with other believers, but they may actively propagate their faith without fear of persecution. Such freedom of religion may be bound up with constitutional free speech clauses or constitutional freedom of religion clauses. Believers may also enjoy some immunity from laws that are otherwise generally applicable (e.g., members of a pacifist religion may be exempt from military service, though required to serve in other ways). Nevertheless believers may not be permitted to appeal to their religion as part of their rationale for voting a certain way or for encouraging others to vote a certain way. For example, if a Christian as a matter of conscience chooses to vote for policies that would ban abortion except where the mother's life is in danger, and wants to persuade others to adopt the same stance, that Christian must not lay out the *religious* reasons for such a stance, because that would be to ignore the constitutional separation of church and state. The sanctions may be social or legal. In other words, the believer under Option Three enjoys a great deal more freedom of religion than the believer under Option One, and is certainly less constrained by demands for privatized religion, but some degree of privatization is still in force. In particular, the religious citizens — whether Christian, Muslim, or Mormon — who oppose abortion are less free to provide their reasons for advocating their position than are citizens who are committed to a naturalistic secularism when they want to give *their* reasons for defending or opposing abortion.

Option Four: In this world, every citizen, religious or otherwise, has the right, indeed the responsibility, to bring to the table of public discussion whatever moral wisdom they can, out of whatever tradition they know. Here there is even more freedom of religion, and correspondingly less imposed privatization. This does not jeopardize the separation of church and state or threaten to establish a religion *in the sense understood when those expressions were coined* (see discussion in chap. 3, summarized below). After all, if, say, Muslims and Christians helped to influence the outcome of an abortion bill, what religion is being established? If one objects because religious motivations are being appealed to in the arena of public legislation, then of course the naturalistic worldview is implicitly being endorsed as the only acceptable one — which means the state has become *anti*-religion in some sense. Some measure of the privatization of religion is being opposed; some curtailment of religious freedom is being adopted. If Christians and other religious citizens cannot participate freely in public discourse, bringing to bear on every discussion whatever insight or wisdom they hold to dearly, they are being relegated to second-class citizenship. It may of course be in their interests to use arguments that are more widely understood in the broader culture: that is a separate issue, an issue of prudence. But if others try to silence them every time they appeal to the categories that are of supreme importance to them, and which they view as part and parcel of elementary faithfulness to the God who redeemed them, then freedom of religion has been severely restricted.[5]

But isn't it the secularists who protect the right to be religious? That is certainly a commonly held view in Western thought. Yet a very strong case can be made, and frequently has been made, for precisely the opposite conclusion. For instance, David Novak persuasively argues that only those whose vision of human rights is grounded in something other and greater than governmental decrees can ever have adequate ground for criticizing government when government becomes repressive. Otherwise the state easily becomes our master instead of our servant. He writes:

> Without such prior obligations and its protections, our rights as humans cannot trump the power of the state because they are derived from that very power that, without true covenant, can easily take away what it has given. So those who would interpret Grotius' dictum literally, that we can have law "even without God" *(etiamsi non sit Deus),* and who claim that de facto atheism is the only cogent basis for commitment to a democratic polity, have no basis for rationally challenging the unjust exercise of state authority,

5. It should be clear that the freedom to speak one's mind openly in the public square does not itself mitigate the responsibility the church always has to be a counter-cultural community. One does not have to adopt the Amish way to be a counter-cultural community.

which is the very antithesis of constitutional democracy. Ironically, those whose god is neither the cosmic order [read "natural law"] nor the orderer of the cosmos [read "God"] have their human rights protected for them by the democratic commitments of those who have a moral religion or a religious morality. But how, then, can our doctrinaire secularists attempt to exclude their very protectors from the conversation any democracy needs to justify its own life and future?[6]

Moreover, the record of the last fifty years or so shows how much Christian appeal was made by African-American leaders of the civil rights movement that finally shamed Jim Crow. Several writers have established in exquisite detail how the driving forces of the movement were not secular white young people (they were added in, as it were) but African-American preachers driven by their understanding of God, human nature, and the Bible.[7] They spoke from *outside* the power structures, for only thus could the power structures be reformed. Do we really want high degrees of privatization in religion and minimal freedom of religion? This is why J. V. Schall can so eloquently warn against "democratic tyranny."[8] This is a new kind of tyranny, he argues, to be placed alongside the more obvious versions generated by Hitler or Stalin. In the West, this kind of tyranny carries a distinctive form: "The danger of democratic tyranny lies in precisely the inability to recognize what is good and what is evil."[9]

A long heritage of reflection argues that if freedom of religion is progressively trimmed, it is only a matter of time before freedom,

6. David Novak, "Law: Religious or Secular?" first published in *Virginia Law Review* (2000), and now conveniently found in Martin Kavka, ed., *Tradition in the Public Square: A David Novak Reader* (Grand Rapids: Eerdmans, 2008), 186.

7. See especially David L. Chappell, *A Stone of Hope: Prophetic Religion and the Death of Jim Crow* (Chapel Hill: University of North Carolina Press, 2007), well reviewed by Elizabeth Fox-Genovese, "Hopeful Pessimism," *Books & Culture* 10, no. 4 (July/August 2004): 8-9; Stephen L. Carter, "Liberalism's Religion Problem," *First Things* 121 (March 2002): 21-32 (an account sometimes truly moving). Cf. also Jean Bethke Elshtain, "The Know-It-All State," *Books & Culture* 6, no. 1 (January/February 2000): 22-23.

8. "A Reflection on the Classical Tractate on Tyranny: The Problem of Democratic Tyranny," *American Journal of Jurisprudence* 41 (1996): 1-19.

9. Schall, "A Reflection on the Classical Tractate on Tyranny," Sect. XI.

more comprehensively envisaged, is also progressively trimmed. It is not for nothing that freedom of religion is often called the first freedom — not merely in historical sequence, but in its foundational power.[10]

Majoritarianism and Democracy

But "democratic tyranny"? Isn't that going a little over the top?

The literature on Christian understanding of the state in general and of democracy in particular is voluminous. I tried to make my own modest contribution to the subject a few years ago[11] and will not repeat the theological arguments and Christian frames of reference

---

10. Some secularists have come to see the need for something like a unified religious vision in the nation if we are to avoid the dangers of an increasingly controlling state, but then try to stipulate the kind of religion it must be. Perhaps the most interesting example is Richard Rorty. At one time he called himself a militant secularist, but from about 1999 on, which marked the publication of his book *Achieving Our Country: Leftist Thought in Twentieth-Century America* (Cambridge: Harvard University Press, 1999), he has advocated what he variously calls "romantic polytheism" or "religion of democracy." The "communion of saints" is displaced by a democratic community, and instead of being energized by truth or God, pragmatists-as-religious-polytheists are energized by social action. We are all polytheists now, Rorty argues, because we are all attracted to various "goods" instead of one ultimate good. He thinks this vision can link together John Stuart Mill, Friedrich Nietzsche, and William James. These "pragmatic theists" must do without a personal God, divine supernatural interventions, personal immortality, the risen Christ, the authority of the Qur'an, and so forth. His vague theism can be tested: if a religious community supports gay marriage and denounces capitalism, then it qualifies as an acceptable religion. And meanwhile teachers at colleges around the country have the religious duty to pressure students who enter as bigoted, homophobic fundamentalists to graduate with the enlightened views of Richard Rorty: college lecturers should do their best to discredit the views of the students' parents, dismissing them as silly. So here is a man who has come to see the importance of a transcendent vision in order to hold state power in check, but wants that vision to be his own, which makes him utterly blind to the fundamental role of religious freedom. He rightly sees the danger of unchecked state power, and knows there must be an extra-state god, but has none to offer but his own views: his own views must be god. The unqualified hubris is mind-boggling, and testifies that he has grasped little of the role of genuine religious freedom in a democracy.

11. D. A. Carson, *Christ and Culture Revisited* (Grand Rapids: Eerdmans, 2008), esp. chaps. 4-5.

here. To prepare the ground for the bearing of *democratic* government on the way we should think about tolerance, however, I must list seven points that I have tried to establish in earlier work, or hinted at earlier in this book, as they form the foundation of what must now be said about tolerance.

(1) In this day of instant polls and few principles, it is easy to think that the way every vote of Congress *should* go is in line with the majority opinion. Certainly the representatives of the people should be sensitive to public opinion, not least majority opinion. Nevertheless, public opinions can be very fickle, easily swayed by dramatic events or by demagogues with golden tongues. Moreover, most polls are notoriously manipulative: one can, in measure, control the outcome by slanting the question. "Do you approve the right of women to decide whether they should have an abortion?" will draw forth a very different percentage than the question "Do you think it is right to kill children in the womb during the third trimester when they are already viable?" Perhaps more importantly, democracy works best when we understand the nature of representative government. No one has said it better than Edmund Burke in his "Speech to the Electors of Bristol" (1744):

> Certainly, gentlemen, it ought to be the happiness and glory of a representative to live in the strictest union, the closest correspondence, and the most unreserved communication with his constituents. Their wishes ought to have great weight with him; their opinion, high respect; their business, unremitted attention. It is his duty to sacrifice his repose, his pleasures, his satisfactions, to theirs; and above all, ever, and in all cases, to prefer their interest to his own. But his unbiassed [*sic*] opinion, his mature judgment, his enlightened conscience, he ought not to sacrifice to you, to any man, or to any set of men living. These he does not derive from your pleasure; no, nor from the law and the constitution. They are a trust from Providence, for the abuse of which he is deeply answerable. Your representative owes you, not his industry only, but his judgment; and he betrays, instead of serving you, if he sacrifices it to your opinion.[12]

12. *The Works of the Right Honourable Edmund Burke*, 6 vols. (London: Henry G. Bohn, 1856-56), 1:446-47.

In short, we are likely to encourage more serious discussion about serious topics if polls are taken less seriously and deliberation is taken more seriously.

(2) "Democracy" is a slippery category. Publications such as those made available year by year by Freedom House remind us how many countries are democratic in the sense that citizens elect their leaders (that is, these countries are electoral democracies), but perhaps not in other senses. Once in, leaders may so control the press and the courts that there is very little freedom. Liberal democracies include constitutional limitations on government, an independent press, an independent judiciary, a reasonably educated citizenship, stable systems for transition of power, equality under the rule of law, a loyal opposition, a significant private sector, freedom of religion and of speech, and minimal corruption. Democratic nations often urge non-democratic nations to become democratic — but if all this means is a vote now and then, there will be very little advance in freedom. The state will still be largely coercive.

In fact, when countries wallow in a miasma of corruption or anarchic violence, democracy may well not be the solution. The indispensable condition for economic stability and some degree of freedom is order. After that, some degree of liberty is needed to galvanize the resources of individual citizens and institutionalize freedom (and with it, stable understandings of tolerance and intolerance at the level of the state).

Two further reflections on democracy constrain our experience of tolerance and intolerance. *First,* a rift has opened up between those who think of democracy as a wonderful servant of a culture that is already committed to external absolutes (whether generated from natural law, the Bible, or ecclesiastical tradition) and others who think of democracy as a neutral political device that makes honest conversation and rational discussion possible among citizens who disagree with one another. Though he tries to be cautious and restrained, Jeffrey Stout is a fine example of the second position, as is Gertrude Himmelfarb,[13] while Gilbert Meilaender and George Weigel exem-

---

13. Jeffrey Stout, *Democracy and Tradition* (Princeton: Princeton University Press, 2005); Gertrude Himmelfarb, *One Nation, Two Cultures* (New York: Knopf, 1999).

plify the first.[14] The fundamental distinction is this: the first view of democracy holds that it works best when it is widely held that people are responsible to truth and morality that stand outside and beyond the decisions of the state; the second view of democracy holds that its genius is essentially independent of the claim of higher obligation or responsibility. It is, in a word, functionally atheistic.

This does *not* mean that all who hold this view are atheists. This needs unpacking a little. Toward the end of World War II, Henri de Lubac persuasively argued that the root cause behind the civilizational crisis that then rocked Europe and much of the rest of the world was what he called "atheistic humanism." This was not mere atheism, but something more complex. Atheists have long expressed their unbelief with various degrees of sophistication and sometimes condescension toward those who do not share their atheism. This, however, was atheistic *humanism* — that is, atheism with a comprehensive vision of what is best for humankind. Marry atheistic humanism and modern technology, de Lubac argued, and it is easy to generate lethal consequences on a massive scale. He wrote, "It is not true, as is sometimes said, that man cannot organize the world without God. What is true is that, without God, he can only organize it against man."[15] What de Lubac had in mind, of course, was primarily Stalinism and the Nazis. But many thinkers, including Solzhenitsyn, have applied the same reasoning to broader movements of Western thought, including the ways in which democracy, stripped of any accountability, easily becomes tyrannous. Europe may be a little farther down this trajectory than the U.S., but it is the same trajectory. Here, too, many people who are believers in some sense treat democracy as a more-or-less neutral political structure for organizing the state in a way that is responsible to people. We do not need to be a nation "under God"; all we need to do is affirm democracy and let the system work. This is a kind of democratic equiva-

14. Gilbert Meilaender, "Talking Democracy," *First Things* 142 (April 2004): 25-30; George Weigel, "Europe's Problem — and Ours," *First Things* 140 (February 2004): 18-25. For a helpful treatment of some aspects of the debate, see Scott H. Moore, *The Limits of Liberal Democracy: Politics and Religion at the End of Modernity* (Downers Grove: InterVarsity, 2009).

15. Henri de Lubac, *The Drama of Atheist Humanism* (London: Sheed & Ward, 1949 [orig. 1944]), 14.

lent of functional atheistic humanism. Sad to tell, many Christians view democracy in the categories of functional atheistic humanism.

In short, "democracy" has quite different sets of associations in the minds of different people.

Second, John O'Sullivan draws attention to a rising paradox:

> The main paradox of current politics is that we are uncritically promoting democracy in the Middle East without apparently noticing that it is increasingly constrained at home by the transfer of power from elected bodies such as Congress to unaccountable institutions such as the courts, federal agencies, and international organizations.[16]

The common ingredient in these transfers of authority is that the authority increasingly comes down from elites rather than up from the people. Historically, liberal democracies understood internationalism to be characterized by power that flows upwards from the democratic nation-state toward international agreements and treaties; in recent decades, the European model, and increasingly the American experience, envisages a kind of trans-nationalism "in which power flows downwards from 'the international community'"[17] — whether (in Europe) the EU, or the International Court, or the UN. The notion that legitimate power does not so much arise out of empirical nation-state democratic peoples but out of an ill-defined and finally unaccountable international community inevitably invites abuse on the part of elites who easily see themselves as superior in insight and understanding: they will interpret the mind of the international community in line with their own ideologies and personal preferences.

Or consider the increasing role the courts play in establishing by judicial fiat what would have in earlier times required legislation.[18]

---

16. John O'Sullivan, "Debating Democracy: Can Everyone Go Athenian?" *National Review* 55, no. 24 (22 December 2003): 36.

17. O'Sullivan, "Debating Democracy," 37.

18. See the two important books edited by Terry Eastland: *Religious Liberty in the Supreme Court: The Cases That Define the Debate over Church and State* (Grand Rapids: Eerdmans, 1995); *Benchmarks: Great Constitutional Controversies in the Supreme Court* (Grand Rapids: Eerdmans, 1995). More broadly, see the trenchant critique by Thomas Sowell, *Intellectuals and Society* (New York: Basic Books, 2009), esp. chap. 6.

The issue is not primarily about whether the federal government through the courts has the right, indeed, the obligation, to bring criminal and other charges against religionists who break the law[19] — surely it does — or even whether it may then use such precedent to pass laws criminalizing behavior which in the past would have been seen as acceptable religious behavior (e.g., publicly affirming that homosexual behavior, even if now not illegal, is nevertheless immoral), thereby reducing freedom of religion. Nor is the issue primarily about the way the Supreme Court regularly "finds" rights in the Constitution that any historical reading of the text could not possibly validate. Nor is it primarily about the way the Court, in its often laudable attempts to adopt a mediating position so as to bring some degree of conciliation to warring factions, can end up using language that actually fosters animus against particular groups.[20] Again, it is not primarily about the way the Court has, since *Everson* in 1947, interpreted the First Amendment as if its religion clauses were at war with each other. The First Amendment reads: "Congress shall make no law respecting an establishment of religion, or prohibiting the free exercise thereof; or abridging the freedom of speech, or of the press; or the right of the people peaceably to assemble, and to petition the Government for a redress of grievances." The two relevant clauses, "Congress shall make no law respecting an establishment of religion" and "or prohibiting the free exercise thereof," are regularly taken by the Court to be at odds with each other, so that the Court's job is to find "neutral" territory between them. But several scholars, especially Carl Esbeck, have shown that both grammatically and in the original intent of the Amendment there are not two competing clauses but one stipulation with two provisions, both of which serve religious freedom.[21] Ori-

19. See especially Marci A. Hamilton, *God vs. the Gavel: Religion and the Rule of Law* (Cambridge: Cambridge University Press, 2005).

20. See the insightful examples and discussion by Steven D. Smith, "Conciliating Hatred," *First Things* 144 (June/July 2004): 17-22.

21. Carl E. Esbeck, "The Establishment Clause as a Structural Restraint on Governmental Power," *Iowa Law Review* 84 (1998): 1-113; idem, "'Play with the Joints between the Religion Clauses' and Other Supreme Court Catachresis," *Hofstra Law Review* 34 (2006): 1331-36. The latter title makes reference to Justice Ruth Bader Ginsburg's opinion that the Court must explore where "there is room for play in the joints between the Clauses" to determine if there is "space for legislative action neither

ginally the no-establishment clause was meant to assure the states that Congress would not interfere with the various establishments of religion already found in the states, and thus worked in tandem with the free-exercise clause to guarantee freedom of religion. The imagined conflict between the parts of the First Amendment is a problem of the Court's creation, and it is fervently to be hoped that the Court will one day extricate itself from its own mess.

For our purposes, however, the *primary* problem is not these various Court decisions, but the fact that the Court has increasingly taken on itself the kinds of roles and decisions that should come through the legislators, the elected representatives. When more and more power devolves to unelected and no-term-limit elites, democracy itself — that is, rule by the people — is weakened.

In short, there are many reasons why what is meant by "democracy" can vary a great deal.

(3) In any case, democracy, however conceived, guarantees neither truth nor morality. People vote out of many different frames of reference. Even when people vote wisely, their representatives frequently change their minds. Alternatively, if the power of the state is increasingly vested in powerful agencies or courts, what the citizens want may matter little — or again, those agencies may sometimes do right things that the citizens do *not* want. All this is a way of saying that a thoughtful Christian cannot possibly elevate democracy to the level of supreme value. Democracy remains the best way of making government more or less accountable. Nevertheless, even when a democratically elected government *is* acting accountably in line with the desires of the majority of the voters, it does not follow that those desires will be for good or wise things. Democracies can believe falsehoods and do cruel and wicked things. No Christian should ever succumb to the idolatrous notion that the right party will bring in utopia. That is not where our ultimate confidence lies.

(4) On the whole, democracies will do better if a majority of their citizens believe that right and wrong exist independently of govern-

---

compelled by the Free Exercise Clause nor prohibited by the Establishment Clause." Cf. also James Hitchcock, "The Enemies of Religious Liberty," *First Things* 140 (February 2011): 26-29.

ment, if they hold they must give an account to God on the last day, and above all if they hold to a robust understanding of the existence of evil and idolatry. That will generate more humility and greater concern to limit how much power is vested in any person or institution.

(5) Democracies become progressively more difficult as their citizens become progressively more polarized. Of course, *every* generation in *every* democracy will be polarized to some extent, not only because various issues will be seen in different ways by different sectors of the populace, but also because competing groups will be vying for power. Add enough polarization, however, and a democracy will drift toward (a) a revolt in the ballot box that brings a reforming group to power; or (b) increasing intrusion by the government into every area of its citizens' lives in order to preserve order where there is no longer a unified vision; or (c) in the worst case, civil war.

(6) This side of the new heaven and the new earth, Christians live in a perennial tension between the demands of God and therefore their responsibilities as citizens of the kingdom of God, and their responsibilities as citizens of a particular state.[22] But they can never forget that the same New Testament that tells us to submit to the state can, under certain circumstances, view the state as beastly. The distance between Romans 13:1-7 and Revelation 13–14 is not very great.

(7) It follows from all that has been said that Christians constitute a community that never quite aligns with the values of the state, including democratic states. Yet if we recall our Master's command to love our neighbors as ourselves, then in democracies we are not limited to the option of deciding at any moment in history whether the state is acting like an unknowing servant of the living God to promote justice and well-being, or rather more like a beast given to tearing Christians apart. No, democracies offer us another option: getting involved and trying to shape things in a way that speaks truth and upholds fundamental distinctions between right and wrong, precisely *because* we love our neighbors. Of course, if the polarizations become too great, we may be dismissed as intolerant people (in the new sense), and laws and judicial decisions may be taken against us. Democracies, too, can become coer-

---

22. For a summary and discussion of the biblical texts that most directly bear on this tension, see Carson, *Christ and Culture Revisited,* 145-203.

cive; "democratic tyranny" is always possible. So be it. We live for the approval of the exalted Christ, not for the approval of polls.

So What Do These Reflections Say about Tolerance and Intolerance?

Although in recent times many Christians have argued that democracy is the best form of government and is finally sanctioned by principles found in Scripture itself, this notion is a modern innovation: no one before the sixteenth century thought this to be the case. Doubtless democracy, especially classic liberal democracy, is the best form of government for establishing at least minimal standards of accountability to the governed and for ensuring smooth (i.e., nonviolent) transitions, but it does not follow that it is always the best regime — and it has the potential for becoming as tyrannous as any other regime *if it begins to think that the systems and structures of democracy are neutral and independent of any greater allegiance.* The thesis of the most recent book by political theorist Francis Fukuyama is right but inadequate: he argues that "successful liberal democracy requires both a state that is strong, unified, and able to enforce laws on its own territory, and a society that is strong and cohesive and able to impose accountability on the state."[23] This thesis does not adequately wrestle with the accountability of citizens (both those in the government and those not in the government) to something — Someone — greater than a political system. When citizens and government officials alike increasingly distance themselves, at least on some issues, from questions of truth and morality, then what the state will and will not *tolerate* easily becomes hijacked by current agendas that may easily become coercive. And if the notion of tolerance itself, in a parallel move, becomes distanced from larger notions of truth and morality, such that in various domains the chief evil is the (new) intolerance, then coercion by the state is bound to follow.[24]

---

23. *The Origins of Political Order: From Prehuman Times to the French Revolution* (New York: Farrar, Straus and Giroux, 2011).

24. One of the more penetrating recent treatments I have seen on the slide from

In short, the well-argued thesis of Robert Kraynak is far superior: *"Thus, we must face the disturbing dilemma that modern liberal democracy needs God, but God is not as liberal or as democratic as we would like Him to be."*[25] Further:

> Christianity is not necessarily a liberal or a democratic religion, nor does it make the support of a political order its *highest* priority. The implications of this dilemma are that the secularists are wrong if they think religion should be kept out of the "public square"; but religious believers are also mistaken if they think that it is easy to reconcile their faith with the principles and practices of modern liberal democracy.[26]

In short, thoughtful Christians who live in democracies, however hard they work at being responsible citizens, cannot possibly imagine that the fact that they live in democracies will protect them from the gyrations currently under way regarding the boundaries — and the very nature — of tolerance and intolerance.

So where do we go from here?

---

truth to feeling, from principle to therapy, from honor to self-esteem, is the recent book by James Bowman, *Honor: A History* (New York: Encounter Books, 2006), esp. chap. 10, "The Aristocracy of Feeling" (pp. 263-91). Bowman begins the chapter by quoting the well-known words of W. H. Auden: "Justice will be replaced by Pity as the Cardinal human virtue, and all fear of retribution will vanish. . . . The New Aristocracy will consist exclusively of hermits, bums, and permanent invalids. The Rough Diamond, the Consumptive Whore, the bandit who is good to his mother . . . will be the heroes and heroines of the New Age, when the general, the statesman, and the philosopher have become the butt of every farce and satire" (from the Christmas oratorio, *For the Time Being* [London: Faber & Faber, 1945], 115-16).

25. Robert Kraynak, *Christianity and Modern Democracy: God and Politics in the Fallen World* (Notre Dame: University of Notre Dame Press, 2001), xiii (emphasis his).

26. Kraynak, *Christianity and Modern Democracy,* xii (emphasis added).

EIGHT

Ways Ahead: Ten Words

—⟋⟋⟍⟍—

The Ten Commandments are often referred to as Ten Words. About the only thing they have in common with the Ten Words I offer here is the number ten. Some of these ten suggestions as to the way ahead will apply most directly to Christians. Some of these suggestions, however, could quite happily be adopted by other people of good will who are more or less convinced by many of the arguments in this book. Readers are welcome to sort out which is which. I should add that my Ten Words vary from the pragmatic to the foundational.

1. Expose the New Tolerance's
Moral and Epistemological Bankruptcy

While acknowledging the small amounts of good that the new tolerance has accomplished, we must constantly expose its moral and epistemological bankruptcy, arguing instead for a return to the older understanding of tolerance. Only that shift will foster rigorous debate about mutually exclusive claims to truth and about competing moral visions. Anything less forecloses on rigorous discussion by branding those who are arguing for this or that corner intolerant.

The issue is not merely theoretical. The older tolerance may well conclude that Pastor Jones's burning of a copy of the Qur'an is foolish and insensitive, but would most likely dismiss him as ridiculous and pretentious rather than giving him all the attention he patently wanted. Moreover, in all fairness, if some imam in Saudi Arabia burned a Bible it is hard to imagine groups of Christians anywhere in the world looking for a mosque to burn: the older tolerance makes a distinction between opinions that may be expressed, however foolish and symbol-laden, and actions of violence and even murder. Freedom of speech is to be cherished, even when it is foolish speech. When Salman Rushdie was knighted, Pakistani Members of Parliament voted unanimously to condemn the award, and one Pakistani cabinet member argued vehemently that this step by the British crown justified not only the attempts to assassinate Rushdie but also any suicide bomber strapping on a bomb vest and killing British citizens. But does that threat mean Christians or Buddhists or secularists are not entitled to say they think that Islam, in some particulars, is deeply wrong or false? Do we instead begin to curb free speech, even foolish speech, on the ground that somebody's feelings are hurt?

Only by keeping the distinction between the old tolerance and the new in mind (even though, as we have seen, they sometimes overlap) will we find the political courage not to be intimidated. Yale University Press offers an excellent example of the direction in which we must *not* go if we wish to adopt the old tolerance and preserve freedoms. The Press commissioned a book on the subject of the cartoons of Muhammad published in Denmark, cartoons to which parts of the Muslim world responded with violence and murder. Written by a respected Brandeis scholar, Jytte Klausen, *The Cartoons That Shook the World*[1] meticulously demonstrates how the crisis was artificially whipped up for political purposes. The really dramatic fact, however, is that Yale yanked the cartoons themselves, refusing to include them in the book but also excluding other representations of Muhammad, such as Gustave Doré's depiction of the Prophet being disemboweled in hell (a scene from Dante's *Inferno*). Why on earth would the cartoons that are the subject of the book not be printed? Would Yale University Press show similar restraint in response to Christian sensitivities? But then again, living in the light of the Western tradition of the old tolerance, Christians would be unlikely to

1. New Haven: Yale University Press, 2009.

threaten the Press or its editors if Jesus were presented in drag and smoking weed, or something similarly outrageous. As far as the Press is concerned, the First Amendment freedoms of speech and of the press are apparently subject to self-imposed limitation on the ground of Muslim veto. It gradually emerged that the decision to publish neither the Danes nor Doré was apparently not so much fear of violence (though that was the official excuse) as pressure from the University not to offend wealthy Muslim benefactors. Mark Steyn is quite right: "Restive European Muslims and unlimited Saudi money can put pressure on American publishers, institutions, and media that will eventually render the First Amendment moot. In Denmark and other countries, craven accommodationists can at least plead that they have incendiary majority-Muslim suburbs with 50 percent youth unemployment. That's not true of New Haven, where the honchos seem to be using fear of violence as a cover for the appetites of their endowment."[2] Whatever the motive, whether fear of violence or fear of losing money, in the name of the new tolerance Yale University Press is sacrificing the old tolerance and thereby jeopardizing the First Amendment freedoms by sacrificing courage and principle on the altar of fear.

We must keep making clear what (old) tolerance consists in, and do what we can to undermine the new tolerance.

2. Preserve a Place for Truth

Another way of making a similar point — that we must insist on the superiority of the old tolerance — is to keep reserving a place for truth, not only in our own hearts and minds, but in our interaction with the broader culture. We can get at this in many ways. Two decades ago, Harold A. Netland usefully distinguished three different contexts in which the notion of tolerance is applicable: the legal, the social, and the intellectual.[3] Netland stresses how Christians ought to

2. Mark Steyn, "Sharia in New Haven," *National Review* 61, no. 16 (7 September 2009): 52.

3. *Dissonant Voices: Religious Pluralism and the Question of Truth* (Grand Rapids: Eerdmans, 1991). More recently, Angus Morrison, "Christian Freedom, Tolerance, and

take the lead in promoting the first two: all people should be treated equally before the law, and because all human beings are made in the image of God, they should all be treated with dignity and respect, not least those with whom we profoundly disagree. As for the intellectual domain, Christians will surely want *tolerance* to operate in the arena of fundamental beliefs. What Netland is saying makes sense, of course, *only* if he is presupposing that an older version of tolerance is in play: we tolerate those whose fundamental beliefs we think are false. The newer version, of course, would insist that it is wrong to say that someone else's fundamental beliefs are false.

Go back two decades earlier yet. In his helpful book *Christ the Controversialist,* John R. W. Stott tells us, first, what Christians should do when they disagree with one another: "The proper activity of professing Christians who disagree with one another is neither to ignore, nor to conceal, nor even to minimize their differences, but to debate them."[4] That of course presupposes a certain view of truth, which happily surfaces elsewhere in his book:

> We seem in our generation to have moved a long way from this vehement zeal for the truth which Christ and his apostles displayed. But if we loved the glory of God more, and if we cared more for the eternal good of the souls of men, we would not refuse to engage in necessary controversy, when the truth of the gospel is at stake. The apostolic command is clear. We are "to maintain the truth in love," being neither truthless in our love, nor loveless in our truth, but holding the two in balance.[5]

Then, to emphasize the importance of truth, he gets at different views of tolerance by distinguishing between a "tolerant mind" and a "tolerant spirit":

> We need to distinguish between the tolerant mind and the tolerant spirit. Tolerant in spirit a Christian should always be, loving, un-

---

the Claims of Truth," *Scottish Bulletin of Evangelical Theology* 17 (1999): 166-69, has expanded the three to four, adding the ecclesiastical.

4. *Christ the Controversialist* (Downers Grove: InterVarsity, 1970), 22.

5. Stott, *Christ the Controversialist,* 19.

derstanding, forgiving and forbearing others, making allowances for them, and giving them the benefit of the doubt, for true love "bears all things, believes all things, hopes all things, endures all things" (1 Corinthians 13:7). But how can we be tolerant in mind of what God has plainly revealed to be either evil or erroneous?[6]

This is a slightly different way of distinguishing between what I have called the old tolerance and the new, but it makes the same point by insisting on the non-negotiability of truth as a category to be maintained, cherished, and upheld.[7] In the much-quoted words of G. K. Chesterton, "The object of opening the mind, as of opening the mouth, is to shut it again on something solid."[8]

Once again, although the issue is in part theoretical, the insistence on truth has many practical applications. It is not only a matter (for Christians) of insisting on the truth of the gospel, but insisting on truthful speech, truthful analyses, truthful representations of other religions (thus claiming they are all saying the same things is *un*truthful, and should be rejected, in the first instance, as untruthful speech), even truthful representations of what the Constitution says (thus if the arguments of Carl Esbeck in the previous chapter are right, the First Amendment means something different from what is commonly assumed: what is the *truth* of the matter?) — and with all of this a willingness, even an eagerness, to correct something we have said if it is persuasively pointed out to us that we have *not* spoken the truth.

3. Expose the New Tolerance's Condescending Arrogance

Engagingly, winsomely, we must keep poking away at the condescending tones of superiority that proponents of the new tolerance

---

6. Stott, *Christ the Controversialist,* 8.

7. Another writer, Stephen McQuoid, makes similar points with different terminology: what I call the old tolerance he calls the true tolerance; see his *The Quest for True Tolerance: Searching for a Tolerance That Does Not Make Society Sick* (Leominster: DayOne, 2008).

8. *The Autobiography,* vol. 16 of *The Collected Works of G. K. Chesterton* (San Francisco: Ignatius, 1998), 212.

keep adopting. To deny categorically that there is a controlling metanarrative is of course as exclusivist as the position of the person who thinks there is such a metanarrative. When Christians make exclusive claims about Christ as the only way to salvation and are therefore condemned as a group for being intolerant, then those who are doing the condemning are of course marginalizing Christians by declaring them to be among the unenlightened, and so are displaying their own intolerance.[9] Similarly, when in the name of international tolerance the West argues that all cultures are of equal value (implicitly denouncing the predations of Western culture in order to adopt a posture of humility), it fails to notice the effect this stance often has. For most cultures think of themselves as worthy, if not superior. To be told by the West that all cultures are of equal value is regularly read as one more intrusive pronouncement from the West designed to diminish all cultures to the same level — so all are insulted by the pronouncement, which is seen as one more evidence of condescending arrogance.

This problem is so deeply intertwined with the new tolerance that we cannot let up on exposing it.

4. Insist That the New Tolerance Is Not "Progress"

We must keep insisting that the notion of progress is far more complex than is usually recognized by those who think that the (new) tolerance marks a high-water mark in civilizational progress. For example, toward the end of the last century the libertarian think tank, the Cato Institute, published a little book, written by Stephen Moore and Julian Simon, with the interesting title, *The Greatest Century That Ever Was: 25 Miraculous Trends of the Past 100 Years*.[10] It reminded us that the end of the nineteenth century was characterized by typhoid and typhus, child labor, horses and their attendant manure, candles,

9. The dogmatism, even the "fundamentalism," of those who are so certain that there can be no certainty about such matters, is treated in an interesting fashion by Stephen Prickett, *Narrative, Religion and Science: Fundamentalism versus Irony, 1700-1999* (Cambridge: Cambridge University Press, 2002).
10. Washington: Cato Institute, 1999.

twelve-hour work days, Jim Crow laws, tenements, slaughterhouses, sanitariums, and outhouses. By the end of the twentieth century, life expectancy had increased by thirty years, the number of cases of deadly disease (tuberculosis, polio, typhoid, whooping cough, and pneumonia) had fallen to fewer than fifty per 100,000, air quality had greatly improved, agricultural productivity had multiplied between five and ten times, the average annual per capita output had risen sevenfold, and real wages had nearly quadrupled. It is hard to deny that progress has been real and measurable. Mind you, all of the evidence adduced is material in nature. The Cato Institute book says nothing about virtue or culture, and fails to mention that the twentieth century has also been the bloodiest in history, characterized by world wars, genocides, and cruelty aided and abetted by technology. It is difficult to see much progress in these domains.

We probably need to go back and read Herbert Butterfield (1900-1979), especially his book *The Whig Interpretation of History*,[11] which tried, however difficult the task may be, to avoid the biases of triumphalism and progressivism in the interpretation of Scripture, to let the evidence speak as carefully and evenhandedly as possible. The greatest danger of an endlessly progressive view of history is the toxic combination of arrogance and self-delusion. We always end up thinking that no one understands anything substantial as well as we do; we talk ourselves into thinking that our stances are the most mature, the most balanced, the most informed. We lose any penetrating grasp of the doctrine of sin and its effects in all of us.

So part of our task, whether in scholarly output or casual speech, is to call into question this delusional supposition that ours is the best society because it is becoming the most tolerant society. The petty gains in open-mindedness that we have achieved in recent decades cannot compare with the staggering losses in clarity as to what tolerance is, in understanding the non-negotiability of truth, in the moral blindness that is rocking our world — a blindness we barely detect.

11. New York: W. W. Norton, 1965 (orig. 1931).

5. Distinguish between Empirical Diversity and the Inherent Goodness of All Diversity

We must distinguish between the reality (often a delightful reality) of empirical diversity and the dogma that diversities of every kind are good.

Reviewing the recent book by Robert D. Putnam and David E. Campbell that analyzes the state of religion in America,[12] R. R. Reno writes:

> Ah, America. Where else in the postmodern West can you find snake-handling preachers; earnest middle-aged women at Unitarian churches who talk about astrology; bookstores full of novels about the rapture; entire seminaries given over to dispensational scholasticism; men with long beards, fur hats, and yarmulkes; priests in cassocks; camp meetings; church suppers with cabbage and lime Jell-O salads; stolid Presbyterians, sweet Methodists, fire-breathing Baptists, and home-schooling Catholics; liberal Jesuits; Jewish Buddhists, Black Muslims, and more — all mixed together in the urban centers, suburban sprawl, and endless rural emptiness of our continent-spanning country?[13]

Multiply this religious diversity by the assorted ethnic, racial, linguistic, economic, and political diversities that characterize not only America but many metropolitan cities in the world today, not to mention the differences in culinary commitments, personal smells and personal hygiene, sense of humor and perceptions of all matters related to sexuality and gender, and the total empirical diversity is everywhere evidenced and part of what drives some toward xenophobia grounded in fear and others toward the new tolerance grounded in sentimental twaddle.

For what we must see is that there is no logical connection from the observation of the undisputed diversity to the entirely disputable dogma that every axis of diversity is equally good. Are the Nazis as good as the Amish?

12. *Amazing Grace: How Religion Divides and Unites Us* (New York: Simon & Schuster, 2010).

13. *First Things* 210 (February 2011): 58.

The same is true of epistemological pluralism. The matter is nicely discussed by Paul Helm:

> We have — I take it — good but not infallible grounds for our views; and others with different beliefs think that they have good but not infallible grounds for their views. And even if some of us have views which are infallibly true, we cannot convince everyone else of the fact. And yet this fact, the fact of epistemological pluralism, does not, or ought not, to lead to [sic] us to think that scepticism is true or even that relativism, the first cousin of scepticism, is true either.
>
> . . . I go along with those who argue that toleration is highly desirable precisely because of our own epistemic fallibilism. Because I may be mistaken in my beliefs, and you may be mistaken in yours, a framework in which our views can be disseminated and argued about is surely something that is of benefit to us both. As a result of such arguments each of us may be able to review his opinions and the reasons that he has for holding them, and the strength with which he holds them. . . . [It] might be argued that toleration is necessary precisely to avoid a collapse into scepticism. Worse, a belief which can only maintain itself by not tolerating its rivals is likely to be viewed sceptically by opponents and cynically by its proponents. We need toleration of diverse opinions to make manifest that there is a spectrum of reasonableness and unreasonableness.[14]

6. Challenge Secularism's Ostensible Neutrality and Superiority

Another way of getting at the last two points is this: we have little choice but to challenge the ostensible neutrality and superiority of contemporary secularism.

Neither secularists of atheistic persuasion, nor theists who have

---

14. Paul Helm, "Rutherford and the Limits of Toleration," in *Tolerance and Truth: The Spirit of the Age or the Spirit of God?* ed. Angus Morrison, Edinburgh Dogmatics Conference Papers (Edinburgh: Rutherford House, 2007), 71.

bought into the thesis that secularism is essentially neutral, should be discouraged from articulating their views, of course. But in this book I have tried to show that as a way of looking at the world secularism is no more neutral than any other ism; indeed, it regularly functions as religions do. Both in the media and in many academic circles, the assumption of the neutrality and intrinsic superiority of secularism is largely taken for granted and is often tied to sloganeering statements regarding the separation of church and state, statements that do not bear up very well under close scrutiny. My point now is that whatever reasonable thing we can do to challenge the ostensible neutrality and superiority of contemporary secularism will in the long haul be good for the nation.

The reason this is important to a discussion of tolerance and intolerance is that in the minds of many people it is this superiority of secularism which, as we have seen, undergirds or even warrants the new tolerance. A few months ago I was in Appleton, Wisconsin, and noticed a "down home"–style restaurant called the Harmony Café. There they posted the following:

Check it at the Door Declaration

I believe:
> that ALL people should be valued and appreciated;
> that every person is a treasure worthy of dignity & respect;
> that diversity in humans is a strength;
> that by pre-judging people and by holding biases,
>> I will miss the beauty within each individual person.

I realize:
> that it is natural for people to be uncomfortable with those
>> who are different
>> from themselves, but I will work to overcome these
>> feelings;
> that people have different abilities, appearances, beliefs,
>> ethnicities, experiences
>> and identities, and I realize that the world is a better place
>> because of
>> these differences.

I pledge:
> to be aware of my biases and the ways I pre-judge people;
> to try to get to know the person who may look, dress, think or
>> live differently
> than I do;
> to check my biases and my temptation to pre-judge people at
> the door.

There is a huge amount of this with which we ought to be in the deepest sympathy. Indeed, at Trinity Evangelical Divinity School I often tell my graduating students that I especially keep on the look-out for students on a pastoral track who can talk to *anybody*. I hope that many such students will choose to serve in our most multicultural cities. Such commitments presuppose an outward-looking, curious, loving stance toward others, a stance all the more reinforced if we believe that every human being has been made in the image of God, that Christ died for sinners like me (and like them), and that God himself regularly chooses the despised people of the world.

And yet, and yet. . . . When we are told that people have different "beliefs" and "identities," and that "the world is a better place because of these differences," are we really to buy into such sweeping declarations? How about the belief that the world would be a better place if all Jews were thrown into the ovens? How about the belief that pedophilia is a fine expression of love? How about the belief that there is nothing morally objectionable about crushing the skull of a baby and sucking out its brains, when in the normal course of events it was only three weeks from birth? How about the dogmatic insistence that all religions are really saying the same thing, even though this belief is terribly insulting to the most devout followers of almost all if not all the major world religions?

Is it really true that all "experiences and identities" make the world "a better place"? How about the experience of being gang-raped? Or of being a repeat sex-offender? Do these experiences make the world a better place? Of course, I still want Christians to be able to talk to anyone, including those who hold to these beliefs or who have experienced these things. But surely that is different from pledging not to "pre-judge" all beliefs and experiences. Some beliefs and experiences *ought* to be "pre-judged."

More importantly, once we have opened up the door to categories like right and wrong, truth and error, then we can no longer escape fundamental questions about what *makes* something right or wrong, true or false — and then we have begun to engage the largest questions of human existence, essentially religious/theological questions. These in turn together remind us afresh that discussions about tolerance and intolerance are valuable *when they are a function of some belief system, some value system,* and not when questions of tolerance and intolerance have been cut off from questions of truth and morality.

This in turn reminds us that we who are Christians have the most powerful reasons for living the self-examined life.[15] We have little credibility when we urge a certain epistemic humility on the part of secularists if we ourselves are not characterized by humility.[16]

7. Practice and Encourage Civility

Christians ought to encourage and practice civility. Such civility is not to be confused with a weakening of Christian convictions or a distinct lack of courage that simply ducks all the hard questions. It means, rather, courtesy, respect, winsomeness, *not least* when we are affirming that another's position is indefensible. It means learning how to dialogue without compromising one's own position. As we saw earlier, a lot of putative interfaith dialogue is in fact a selling of the pass: we might call it *inter-non-faith* dialogue. But there are some excellent examples of real interfaith dialogue,[17] and they ought to be multiplied.

There are appropriate times and places for moral outrage, but those who go through life making moral outrage their specialty con-

15. Cf. Os Guinness, *Unspeakable: Facing Up to the Challenge of Evil* (New York: HarperOne, 2006).

16. See the delightful book by C. J. Mahaney, *Humility: True Greatness* (Sisters: Multnomah, 2005).

17. Not least the important book by Timothy C. Tennent, *Christianity at the Religious Roundtable: Evangelicalism in Conversation with Hinduism, Buddhism, and Islam* (Grand Rapids: Baker, 2002).

vince no one but their followers, and certainly do not commend the Lord Jesus who, though he could on occasion blister hypocritical opponents of the dawning kingdom of God, was also known to weep over the city.[18]

8. Evangelize

Evangelize. Evangelize and plant churches. Evangelize and pray. Evangelize and live life in the light of the consummated kingdom for which we wait. Evangelize.

One might well ask how or why this point should feature in a book trying to sort out the complex currents swirling around the notions of tolerance and intolerance. There are at least four reasons.

First, openly declaring the gospel to others in an effort to win them to Jesus Christ constitutes a reminder, both for ourselves and for others, that the gospel is supremely important. One of the dangers of a book like this is that its author and readers may begin to think that forging a more responsible track toward older or classic tolerance is one of the most important activities, if not *the* most important activity, in which we could be engaged. It is not. If we treat it as if it were, we begin to act like functional atheists ourselves.

Second, if we ourselves are evangelizing we shall have many opportunities to explain what we think evangelism is or should be. By and large the press will tar every effort at evangelism with the label "proselytism," as we have already seen. But this provides us with an opportunity to insist on the different word associations that "proselytism" and "evangelism" have for Christians. The former is unworthy witness, the attempt to win others to our position out of unworthy or even corrupt motives. By contrast, to evangelize is (in the words of the *Manila Manifesto*) "to make an open and honest statement of the gospel, which leaves the hearers entirely free to make up their own minds about it." If others willfully confuse the two, there is not much we can

---

18. One need not agree with every judgment in the book to recognize that the appeal of Richard J. Mouw, *Uncommon Decency: Christian Civility in an Uncivil World,* 2nd ed. (Downers Grove: InterVarsity, 2010), is both moving and penetrating.

do about it — but we should be bold not only to engage in evangelism but to make clear what it is and isn't.

Third, when we evangelize, we have opportunity to explain why genuine freedom of religion necessarily includes the right to evangelize (on the part of the witness) and the right to change to another religion or to no religion (or away from no religion). Earlier chapters have briefly indicated how many voices there are that want to eliminate this element of freedom of religion, arguing that all forms of evangelism/proselytism necessarily involve telling others where they are wrong, which is intolerant. We insist that genuine tolerance can be maintained only if people have the right — indeed, the responsibility — to tell others where they think they are wrong, in an effort to win them to a different direction.

Fourth, if men and women are genuinely converted (as opposed to making an innocuous decision that affects little of their thinking and priorities, which from a biblical perspective is no conversion at all), they will become salt in a decaying world, light in a dark world — and their influence in turn, in God's mercy, may turn the tide of public perception. Most emphatically this does *not* mean that we should be seeking to win people to Christ because it will make America (or Canada or Britain or France or Brazil or China or whatever) a better place. That sounds too much like a purely utilitarian and materialistic view of faith in Christ Jesus. Yet when the gospel truly does take hold in any culture, changes in that culture are inevitable. That is why in China today, while some voices are adamantly resolved to diminish the influence of Christianity, other voices are eager for Christians to take their place in society because so often Christians are the best workers, the most honest and incorruptible employees, and so forth. There are even moves to study Christianity more closely, with these economic and utilitarian purposes in mind. Of course, at one level these moves reflect a profound misapprehension as to what is of fundamental importance in Christianity — but at least the potential positive impact of many conversions to Christ is thereby implicitly affirmed.

9. Be Prepared to Suffer

Be prepared to suffer. Here three things must be said.

First, the New Testament devotes quite a lot of space to telling Christ's followers that suffering for Jesus' sake should be seen as the norm rather than the exception. Our identity with Jesus will win for us from the world the same response the world has for Jesus (John 15:18-25). Doubtless that is why the apostle Paul insists that God gives Christians *two* gracious gifts: faith, and suffering for Jesus' sake (Philippians 1:29). We delight to receive the faith; we ought similarly to delight in being associated with Jesus' sufferings (Philippians 3:10). So it was with the apostles who rejoiced when they were counted worthy to suffer disgrace for the Name (Acts 5:41). Our attitude to being the butt of intolerance, not least when such intolerance is displayed in the name of tolerance, ought to be one of quiet joy — not because we are masochists, but because it is such a privilege to be associated with the name of Jesus.

Second, if the arguments of this book are right with respect to how we should view democracy, we should not be surprised when democracy becomes tyrannous. Just as Christians cannot finally serve both God and Money, so they cannot owe ultimate allegiance to the kingdom of God and to an earthly democracy. God is not establishing a democratic republic, but an eternal kingdom in a new heaven and a new earth.

Third, if something more than sneering condescension should be imposed on Christians in Western countries, it will not come in a sudden, massive decree: "All Christians must be arrested and incarcerated immediately as enemies of the state." It is far more likely to come incrementally and *in the name of preserving tolerance.* For example, in the U.S., two states have already passed laws stating that employees of Christian institutions who are not themselves teaching the Bible or theology cannot be fired because (for instance) it becomes known that they are practicing homosexuals. The teachers of the Bible and theology *may* be fired, because the administrators of the institution may rightly appeal to the First Amendment, but if the workers cut the grass or keep the books, there is no First Amendment protection for the institution. So far this has not been tested by the Supreme

Court. But if the Court were to allow such legislation to stand, major seminaries could be fined into bankruptcy and their officers go to prison. The same legislation might then be extended to, say, church musicians, but not the clergy. And so on, and so on. The rationale for this prosecution (and persecution), of course, would be that the state cannot tolerate the intolerance of these Christians. And were this to happen, we would gladly bear it, and learn a little better how to do evangelism in our prisons.

10. Delight in and Trust God

Delight in God, and trust him. God remains sovereign, wise, and good. Our ultimate confidence is not in any government or party, still less in our ability to mold the culture in which we live. God may bring about changes that reflect the more robust understanding of tolerance better known in earlier times, and that would be very helpful; alternatively, he may send "a powerful delusion so that [people] will believe the lie" (2 Thessalonians 2:11), and in consequence we may enter into more suffering for Jesus than the West has known for some time. That would have the effect of aligning us with brothers and sisters in Christ in other parts of the world, and enable us to share something of the apostles' joy (Acts 5:41).

Index of Names

———◈◈◈———

Index of Subjects

Index of Scripture References

—⁓ᨒᨒ⁓—